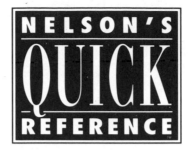

BIBLE MAPS
AND CHARTS

THOMAS NELSON PUBLISHERS
Nashville • Atlanta • London • Vancouver

© 1994 by Thomas Nelson, Inc.

Published in Nashville, Tennessee, by Thomas Nelson, Inc.

Library of Congress Cataloging-in-Publication Data

Bible maps & charts.
        p.   cm. — (Nelson's Quick reference)
    Includes index.
    ISBN 0-8407-6908-3
    1. Bible—Handbooks, manuals, etc. 2. Bible—
eography—Maps. 3. Bible—Chronology—Charts, diagrams,
etc. I. Thomas Nelson Publishers. II. Title: Bible maps and
charts. III. Series.
BS417.B52 1994
220'.021—dc20   93–44228
                                                                CIP

Printed in the United States of America
1 2 3 4 5 6 7 8 — 00 99 98 97 96 95 94

CONTENTS

♦

PREFACE

♦

What this book contains and does

Nelson's Quick-Reference™ Bible Maps and Charts offers you over three hundred visual resources for use with your Bible. Selected from Thomas Nelson's Bibles and reference books, these fine-quality maps and informative charts and tables help make any Bible a *study* Bible. An overview chart and succinct listing of landmarks for each book of the Bible help you survey the lay of the land for all sixty-six books of the Old and New Testaments. These basics are then supplemented by

Timelines that help you relate a person, book, or event to the dates of other well-known persons or events—to help you organize the details into a well-connected flow (see "The Times of the Prophets," p. 135; note that almost all dates given in timelines are approximate);

Several kinds of *maps:*
- maps showing *geographical features*—to help you imagine the physical stage upon which the dramas of Scripture were played (see "Palestine: Physical Regions," p. 15);
- maps tracing the *journeys or actions* of specific Bible personalities—to help you recount these events with a greater sense of their reality (see "Route of the Jews' Return from Exile," p. 105);
- and maps showing the *changing political boundaries* of the kingdoms and empires that influenced the course of

biblical history—to help you see how Israel of Bible times both prospered and suffered and how the earliest Christians spread the gospel from Jerusalem throughout the lands touched by the Mediterranean Sea (see "The Persian Empire—500 B.C.," p. 106, and "Herod's Kingdom at Jesus' Birth," p. 208);

Several kinds of *charts and tables:*

• charts that *summarize* biblical information in a form that is easy to read and remember (see, "Mentioned First in Genesis," p. 7);

• charts that *compare and contrast* aspects of Bible personalities (see "Contrasting Jonah and the Mariners," p. 170), the teachings of Bible books (see "Contrasts Between Chronicles and Samuel—Kings," p. 92), or interpretations of evangelical students of the Bible (see "Interpretations of Revelation 20:1–6," p. 325);

• charts that *classify* important Bible information—to help you *simplify and master* a large body of information in a useful fashion (see "Types of Psalms," p. 122);

• and illustrations that *show* important items (see, "The Furniture of the Tabernacle," p. 28).

How to use this book

Nelson's Quick-Reference™ Bible Maps and Charts is easy to use. Because it is organized by Bible book—from Genesis through Revelation—you can look up the Bible book you are reading in the Table of Contents and turn immediately to find the maps and charts provided there. But there's more. By using the alphabetical Index at the back of the book, you can look up other maps and charts related to the book or topic you are studying. One other tip:

Because the arrangement of the Bible is *in general* chronological, you may want to look at the resources provided for
books near the book you are studying. For example, when
studying the Gospel of Mark, look up resources provided
for the Gospels of Matthew, Luke, and John as well. And
whenever your present study brings up other names or
events, you can look these up through the Table of Contents and the Index. For example, while studying the
prophecy of Daniel, you may use the chart "Dreams and
Visions in Daniel," p. 154. There you will notice the
kingdoms of Babylon, (Medo-)Persia, Greece, and Rome
listed. You may be interested in seeing a map that shows
each kingdom and can find one of each by using the Index.

However you wish to use these maps, charts, and illustrations, together they provide you with an interesting
visual companion to the Bible. *Nelson's Quick-Reference™
Bible Maps and Charts* can help you understand Bible
truths better and remember them more easily and
vividly—and stimulate you to your own discoveries and
insights in Bible study, whether by yourself or in a group.
We hope you will find that, in your use of *Nelson's Quick-
Reference™ Bible Maps and Charts,* seeing it helps you believe it!

PART ONE

♦

THE OLD TESTAMENT

ONE

BOOKS OF THE LAW

♦

Book	Genesis	Exodus	Leviticus	Numbers	Deuteronomy
Key Idea	Beginnings	Redemption	Worship	Wandering	Renewed Covenant
The Nation	Chosen	Delivered	Set Apart	Directed	Made Ready
The People	Prepared	Redeemed	Taught	Tested	Retaught
God's Character	Powerful Sovereign	Merciful	Holy	Just	Loving Lord
God's Role	Creator	Deliverer	Sanctifier	Sustainer	Rewarder
God's Command	"Let there be!"	"Let My people go!"	"Be holy!" `	"Go in!"	"Obey!"

Old Testament Overview

Persons	Periods and Events	Contemporary Cultures	Old Testament Books Written
Adam	BEFORE THE PATRIARCHS Creation Flood	Prehistorical Era	
Abraham, Isaac, Jacob, Joseph	PATRIARCHS Abraham enters the land c. 2090 B.C. Joseph Prime Minister c. 1885–1805	Patriarchal Narratives reflect culture of Mesopotamia and Egypt	Job?
	EGYPTIAN SOJOURN c. 1875–1445	Egypt enslaves the Israelites	
Moses	WILDERNESS WANDERING c. 1445–1405		Genesis, Exodus, Leviticus, Numbers, Deuteronomy
Joshua, Deborah, Gideon, Jephthah, Samson	CONQUEST AND JUDGES c. 1405–1050	Palestine occupied, various nations oppress Israel	Joshua, Judges
Samuel, Saul, David, Solomon	UNITED MONARCHY Established 1050	Surrounding nations defeated by Israel	Ruth, Samuel, Psalms, Song of Solomon, Proverbs, Ecclesiastes

DIVIDED MONARCHY
931–722 Divided 931

SOUTH:
Rehoboam
Jehoshaphat
Uzziah

NORTH:
Jeroboam I
Ahab
Jeroboam II

Aramean Kingdom 931–732

Obadiah, Joel
Jonah, Amos, Hosea, Isaiah, Micah

Hezekiah

Fall of Aram c. 732
Assyrian domination of Palestine 745–650

Nahum, Zephaniah

Fall of Samaria c. 722

JUDAH ALONE 722–586

Josiah

Daniel's Captivity
Ezekiel's Captivity

Jeremiah, Lamentations, Habakkuk, Kings, Daniel, Ezekiel

Jeremiah

Fall of Jerusalem c. 586

Babylonian Supremacy 625–539
Medo-Persian Rule 539–331

Zerubbabel
Haggai
Zechariah

RESTORATION 538–c. 400
Second Temple

Haggai, Zechariah

Ezra's Return c. 458

Chronicles, Ezra, Esther

Malachi

Nehemiah's Return c. 444

Nehemiah, Malachi

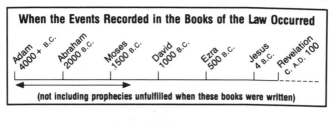

When the Events Recorded in the Books of the Law Occurred

Adam 4000 + B.C. | Abraham 2000 B.C. | Moses 1500 B.C. | David 1000 B.C. | Ezra 500 B.C. | Jesus 4 B.C. | Revelation C. A.D. 100

(not including prophecies unfulfilled when these books were written)

The Book of GENESIS

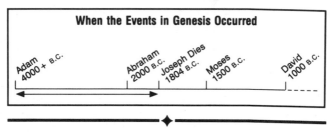

When the Events in Genesis Occurred

Adam 4000 + B.C. | Abraham 2000 B.C. | Joseph Dies 1804 B.C. | Moses 1500 B.C. | David 1000 B.C.

LANDMARKS OF GENESIS

Key Word: *Beginnings*

Genesis gives the beginning of almost everything, including the beginning of the universe, life, humanity, sabbath, death, marriage, sin, redemption, family, literature, cities, art, language, and sacrifice.

Key Verses: *Genesis 3:15; 12:3*

Key Chapter: *Genesis 15*

Central to all of Scripture is the Abrahamic Covenant, which is given in 12:1–3 and ratified in 15:1–21. Israel

Overview of Genesis

FOCUS	Four Events				Four People			
REFERENCE	1:1 ——	3:1 ——	6:1 ——	10:1 ——	12:1 ——	25:19 ——	27:19 ——	37:1 ——50:26
DIVISION	Creation	Fall	Flood	Nations	Abraham	Isaac	Jacob	Joseph
	Human Race				Hebrew Race			
TOPIC	Historical				Biographical			
LOCATION	Fertile Crescent (Eden-Haran)				Canaan (Haran-Canaan)			Egypt (Canaan-Egypt)
TIME	c. 2000 Years c. 4000+-c. 2166 B.C.				281 Years c. 2166-1885 B.C.			81 Years (1885-1804 B.C.)

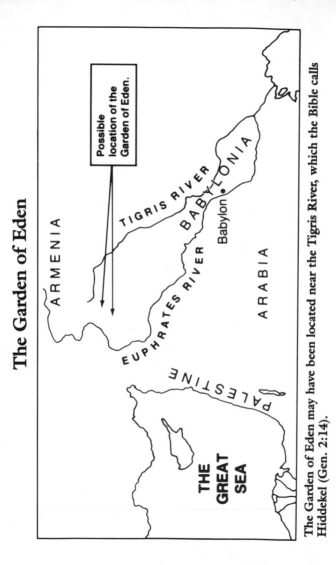

The Garden of Eden

Possible location of the Garden of Eden.

ARMENIA

TIGRIS RIVER

BABYLONIA

Babylon •

EUPHRATES RIVER

ARABIA

PALESTINE

THE GREAT SEA

The Garden of Eden may have been located near the Tigris River, which the Bible calls Hiddekel (Gen. 2:14).

receives three specific promises: (1) *the promise of a great land*—"from the river of Egypt to the great river, the River Euphrates" (15:18); (2) *the promise of a great nation*—"and I will make your descendants as the dust of the earth" (13:16); and (3) *the promise of a great blessing*—"I will bless you and make your name great; and you shall be a blessing" (12:2).

◆

The Creative Work of God

	Genesis 1	Genesis 2
Creation Accounts	God the Creator	God the covenant-keeper
	Elohim	YAHWEH
	God as powerful	God as personal
	Creation of the universe	Creation of man
	Climaxes with man	Climaxes with marriage
	The six days of creation	The sixth day of creation
Genesis 1:2	"without form . . ."	". . . and void"
Six Days of Creation	In the first three days, God shaped the creation	In the second three days, God populated the creation
	Day 1: light	Day 4: sun, moon, stars
	Day 2: water, atmosphere	Day 5: sea creatures, birds
	Day 3: earth, vegetation	Day 6: animals

Mentioned First in Genesis

Altar	8:20	Cave dweller	19:30
Angel	16:7	Chariot	41:43
Archer	21:20	Child	11:30
Bird	1:21	Child named before birth	16:11
Camp	32:2	City builder	4:17

The Abrahamic Covenant

Genesis 12:1–3   God initiated His covenant with Abram when he was living in Ur of the Chaldeans, promising a land, descendants, and blessing.

Genesis 12:4, 5   Abram went with his family to Haran, lived there for a time, and left at the age of 75.

Genesis 13:14–17   After Lot separated from Abram, God again promised the land to him and his descendants.

Genesis 15:1–21   This covenant was ratified when God passed between the sacrificial animals Abram laid before God.

Genesis 17:1–27   When Abram was 99 God renewed His covenant, changing Abram's name to Abraham ("father of a multitude"). Sign of the covenant: circumcision.

Genesis 22:15–18   Confirmation of the covenant because of Abraham's obedience.

The Abrahamic covenant was foundational to the other covenants:

- The promise of *land* in the Palestinian Covenant (Deut. 30:1–10)
- The promise of *kingly descendants* in the Davidic Covenant (2 Sam. 7:12–16)
- The promise of *blessing* in the "Old" and "New" Covenants (Ex. 19:3–6; Jer. 31:31–40)

Key Places in the Lives of the Patriarchs

Maps on the following pages show many of these locations, where key events of early biblical history occurred.

Abraham (Abram)

Ur—Abram's birthplace

Haran—Abram dwells with father Terah, nephew Lot, and wife Sarai.

Shechem—Abram builds an altar at the terebinth tree of Moreh (Gen. 12:6, 7).

Bethel—Abram builds another altar at "the mountain east of Bethel" (Gen. 12:8).

Mt. Moriah—Abraham put to the test with Issac (Gen. 22; location uncertain).

Mamre—Abraham buried in the cave of Machpelah near Mamre (Gen. 25:9, 10).

Isaac

Beersheba—Isaac lives his life in one region, southern Canaan.

The Nations of Genesis 10

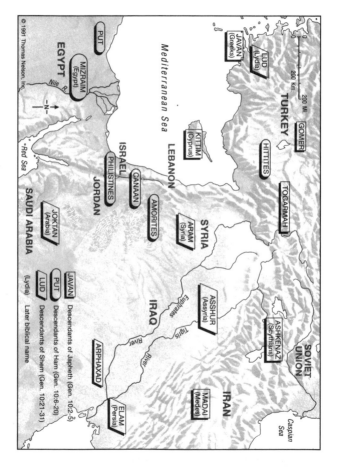

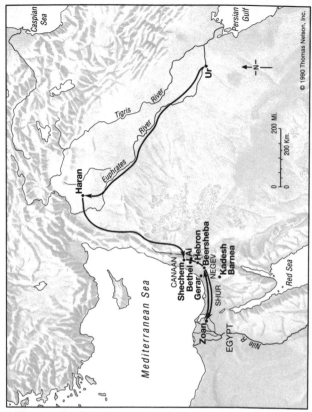

Abraham's Journey of Faith

Abraham's 1,500-mile journey was fueled by faith. "And he went out, not knowing where he was going. By faith he dwelt in the land of promise as in a foreign country, . . . for he waited for the city which has foundations, whose builder and maker is God" (Heb. 11:8–10).

Jacob

Beersheba—Born to Isaac and Rebekah; Jacob tricks Esau into trading his birthright for a meal (Gen. 25:24–34).

Bethel—Jacob travels to his ancestral homeland of Haran to see his uncle Laban and find a wife; at Bethel he dreams about angels going up and down a ladder and receives assurance of God's blessings (Gen. 28:1–19).

Haran—Jacob serves Laban for fourteen years, marrying Leah, then Rachel (Gen. 29:15–28).

Penuel—Returning from Haran, Jacob wrestles with an

Jacob Returns to Canaan
(Genesis 32)

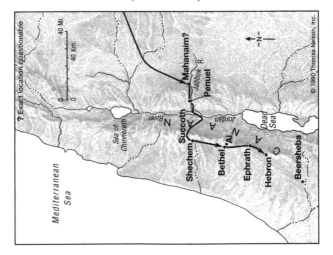

angel at the River Jabbok. God changes his name to Israel (Gen. 32:22–32).

Egypt—Jacob travels with his family to escape a famine in Canaan (Gen. 46:1–6); in Egypt, blessed his twelve sons just before his death (Gen. 49:1–33).

Mamre—Jacob's body returned to Canaan from Egypt and buried in the family plot in the cave of Machpelah, near Mamre (Gen. 50:13, 14).

Joseph

Dothan—Joseph follows his shepherd brothers from Hebron to Dothan, where they sell him to merchants in Egypt.

Joseph's Journey Into Egypt
(Genesis 37)

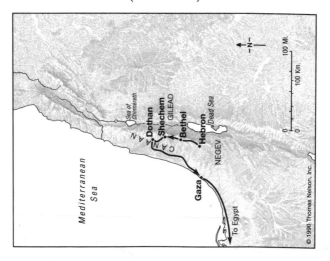

Egypt—Joseph, after great adversity, becomes second in
    command and provides refuge for Jacob and his fam-
    ily from famine (Gen. 46). Joseph dies in Egypt.

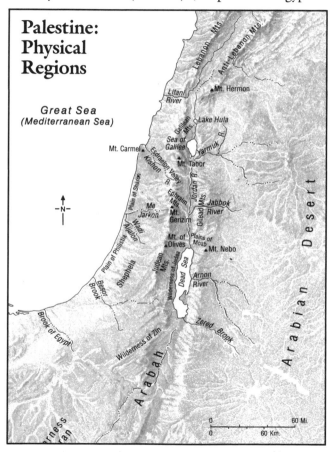

Palestine: Physical Regions

Great Sea
(Mediterranean Sea)

Lebanon Mts.

Anti-Lebanon Mts.

Litani River

▲ Mt. Hermon

Galilee Mts.

Lake Hula

Sea of Galilee

Mt. Carmel ▲

Esdraelon Valley

Yarmuk R.

Kishon R.

▲ Mt. Tabor

Plain of Sharon

Ephraim Mts.

Jordan R.

Jabbok River

Me Jarkon

Mt. Gerizim

Gilead Mts.

Wadi Aijalon

Mt. of Olives ▲

Plains of Moab

▲ Mt. Nebo

Plain of Philistia

Judean Mts.

Shephela

Wilderness of Judea

Dead Sea

Arnon River

Besor Brook

Brook of Egypt

Wilderness of Zin

Arabah

Zered Brook

Arabian Desert

—N—

0 ————— 60 Mi.
0 ————— 60 Km.

Spiritual Contrasts
in the Patriarchal Age

First Generation	Second Generation	Third Generation	Fourth Generation
Abraham	Ishmael and Isaac	Esau and Jacob	Joseph and his eleven brothers
Abraham: man of faith believed in God	Ishmael: not son of promise Isaac: called on God believed God	Esau: unspiritual little faith Jacob: at first compromised, later turned to the Lord	Joseph: man of God showed faith Brothers: treachery, immorality, lack of separation from Canaanites
Abraham: built altars to God (Gen. 12:7, 8; 13:4, 18; 22:9)	Isaac: built an altar to God (Gen. 26:25)	Jacob: built altars to God (Gen. 33:20; 35:1, 3, 7)	No altars were built to God in the fourth generation

Old Testament Dreams and Visions

Personality	Message of Dream or Vision	Biblical Reference
DREAMS		
Jacob	Assurance of God's covenant	Gen. 28:10–15
Joseph	Joseph's future prominence over his brothers	Gen. 37:1–11
Solomon	Assurance of God's wisdom	1 Kin. 3:5–10
VISIONS		
Jacob	Instructed to go to Egypt	Gen. 46:2–4
Isaiah	A revelation of God's holiness	Is. 6:1–8

| Ezekiel | God's promise to restore His people Israel | Ezek. 37 |
| Daniel | The great world powers to come and the glories of Christ | Dan. 7; 8
Dan. 10:5–9 |

In Old Testament times, God often used dreams (when a person was asleep) and visions (when a person was awake) to make His will known. The Egyptian Pharaoh's dream could not be interpreted by his magicians. But Joseph told him that it referred to a forthcoming period of famine in the land (Gen. 41).

The Angel of the Lord

The Angel (or ''Messenger'') of the Lord in the Old Testament is a mysterious messenger of God. The Lord used this heavenly emissary to appear to human beings who otherwise would not be able to see Him and live (Ex. 33:20). The Angel of the Lord performed actions associated with God, such as revelation, deliverance, and God's judgment. This has led many to believe that the Angel of the Lord is a Christophany, i.e., an appearance of Christ in the Old Testament. The Angel of the Lord appeared to the following personalities and performed the following actions on God's behalf.

Appeared to	Action	Biblical Reference
Hagar	Instructed Hagar to return to Sarah and told her she would have many descendants	Gen. 16:7–10
Abraham	Prevented Abraham from sacrificing his son Isaac	Gen. 22:11–13

Jacob	Wrestled with Jacob through the night and blessed him at daybreak	Gen. 32:24–30
Moses	Spoke to Moses from the burning bush, promising to deliver the Israelites from enslavement	Ex. 3:1–8
Israelites	Protected the children of Israel from the pursuing Egyptian army	Ex. 14:19, 20
Israelites	Prepared the children of Israel to enter the Promised Land	Ex. 23:20–23
Balaam	Blocked Balaam's path, then sent him to deliver a message to Balak	Num. 22:22–35
Joshua	Reassured Joshua, in his role as commander of the army of the Lord	Josh. 5:13–15
Israelites	Announced judgment against the Israelites for their sinful alliances with the Canaanites	Judg. 2:1–3
Gideon	Commissioned Gideon to fight against the Midianites	Judg. 6:11–24
Elijah	Provided food for Elijah in the wilderness	1 Kin. 19:4–8
David	Appeared to David on the threshing floor of Ornan, where David built an altar	1 Chr. 21:16–22
Residents of Jerusalem	Delivered the citizens of this city from the Assyrian army	Is. 37:36
Shadrach, Meshach, and Abed-Nego	Protected these young Israelites from Nebuchadnezzar's fiery furnace in Babylon	Dan. 3:25
The Temple	The "Messenger of the Covenant" coming in judgment	Mal. 3:1

The Book of
EXODUS

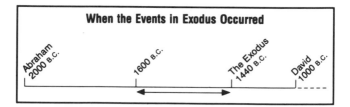

When the Events in Exodus Occurred

Abraham 2000 B.C. — 1600 B.C. — The Exodus 1440 B.C. — David 1000 B.C.

Egyptian Pharaohs

"Pharaoh" means "great house" and refers to the king who lived in the "great house." The pharaoh at the time of Moses' birth was probably Amenhotep I or Thutmose I.

Ahmosis I	1570–46 B.C.	Amenhotep IV	1379–62 B.C.
Amenhotep I	1546–26 B.C.	Smenkhkare	1364–61 B.C.
Thutmose I	1526–12 B.C.	Tutankhamon	1361–52 B.C.
Thutmose II	1512–04 B.C.	Ay	1352–48 B.C.
Thutmose III	1504–1450 B.C.	Horemheb	1348–20 B.C.
Hatshepsut	1504–1483 B.C.	Rameses I	1320–18 B.C.
Amenhotep II	1450–25 B.C.	Seti I	1318–04 B.C.
Thutmose IV	1425–17 B.C.	Rameses II	1304–1236 B.C.
Amenhotep III	1417–1379 B.C.	Merneptah	1236–1223 B.C.

Overview of Exodus

FOCUS	Redemption from Egypt			Revelation from God	
REFERENCE	1:1 ——— 2:1 ———	5:1 ———	15:22 ———	19:1 ———	32:1 ——— 40:38
DIVISION	The Need for Redemption	The Preparation for Redemption	The Redemption of Israel	The Preservation of Israel	The Revelation of the Covenant	The Response of Israel to the Covenant
TOPIC	Subjection	Narration	Redemption		Legislation Instruction	
LOCATION	Egypt		Wilderness	Mount Sinai		
TIME	430 Years		2 Months	10 Months		

Moses' Flight & Return to Egypt
(Exodus 2—4)

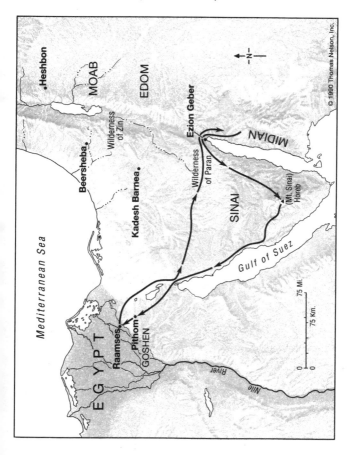

LANDMARKS OF EXODUS

Key Word: *Redemption*

Central to the Book of Exodus is the concept of redemption. Israel was redeemed *from* bondage in Egypt and *into* a covenant relationship with God.

Key Verses: *Exodus 6:6; 19:5, 6*

Key Chapters: *Exodus 12—14*

The climax of the entire Old Testament is recorded in chapters 12—14: the salvation of Israel through blood (the Passover) and through power (the Red Sea).

Moses the Deliverer

With the phrase "there arose a new king over Egypt who did not know Joseph" (Ex. 1:8), the stage is set for the need for a deliverer. With Pharaoh Ahmosis I (see chart p. 23) came the establishment of an eighteenth Egyptian dynasty and a series of rulers who did not honor the relationship that had been established with Joseph in Egypt. Born in Egypt to slave parents from the house of Levi, Moses spent his youth in the Pharaoh's royal household, probably at Thebes. Formal education was a social privilege; in addition to reading and writing, he probably learned mathematics and music. But after he discovered the plight of his own people, at the age of forty he killed an Egyptian and was forced to flee to the land of Midian. There he had a dramatic encounter with God in the burning bush. Moses would be trained in the solitude of the desert for forty more years, before he returned to Pharaoh's court to be God's appointed deliverer for this people.

The Ten Plagues on Egypt
(Exodus 7—12)

Scholars have noted that the plagues sent by the God of Moses and Aaron correspond to gods the Egyptians worshiped. The contest between Moses and the Pharaoh was a power encounter in which Yahweh demonstrated His complete mastery, hardening the Pharaoh's heart as easily as He sent fearsome plagues, all to accomplish His will of liberating His people.

The Plague	Egyptian God	The Effect
1. Blood (7:20)	Hapi	Pharaoh hardened (7:22)
2. Frogs (8:6)	Heket	Pharaoh begs relief, promises freedom (8:8), but is hardened (8:15)
3. Lice (8:17)	Hathor Nut	Pharaoh hardened (8:19)
4. Flies (8:24)	Shu Isis	Pharaoh bargains (8:28), but is hardened (8:32)
5. Livestock diseased (9:6)	Apis	Pharaoh hardened (9:7)
6. Boils (9:10)	Sekhmet	Pharaoh hardened (9:12)
7. Hail (9:23)	Geb	Pharaoh begs relief (9:27), promises freedom (9:28), but is hardened (9:35)

8. Locusts (10:13)	Serapis	Pharaoh bargains (10:11), begs relief (10:17), but is hardened (10:20)
9. Darkness (10:22)	Ra	Pharaoh bargains (10:24), but is hardened (10:27)
10. Death of firstborn (12:29)		Pharaoh and Egyptians beg Israel to leave Egypt (12:31–33)

The Exodus from Egypt
(Exodus 12—40; Leviticus 1—19)

The precise route taken by the Israelites to Mt. Sinai after their departure from Egypt is uncertain. As the map indicates, scholars have proposed both northern and southern routes, with the southern path the most likely. It took approximately two months to reach Sinai, where the Israelites encamped for roughly ten months during the period of divine revelation.

The Ten Commandments
(Exodus 20; also Deuteronomy 5)

After the deliverance from Egypt, God led His people to Mt. Sinai, where He gave Moses the Law on the stone tablets. The Ten Commandments focus on our relationship to God and our relationship to others.

Relationship to God

1. You shall have no other Gods before Me.
2. You shall not make for yourself a carved image (idol) . . . [nor] bow down nor serve them.

The Exodus from Egypt

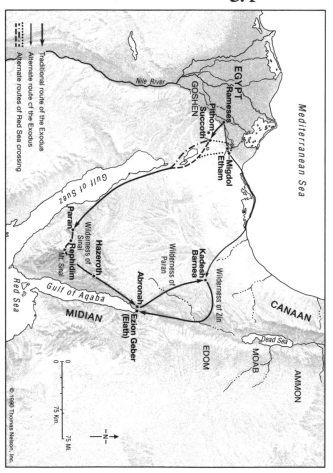

3. You shall not take the name of the LORD your God in vain.
4. Remember the Sabbath day, to keep it holy.

Relationship to Others

5. Honor your father and your mother, that your days may be long upon the land.
6. You shall not murder.
7. You shall not commit adultery.
8. You shall not steal.
9. You shall not bear false witness.
10. You shall not covet.

The Plan of the Tabernacle
(Exodus 24—27)

The tabernacle was to provide a place where God might dwell among His people. The term *tabernacle* sometimes refers to the tent, including the holy place and the Most Holy, which was covered with embroidered curtains. But in other places it refers to the entire complex, including the curtained court in which the tent stood.

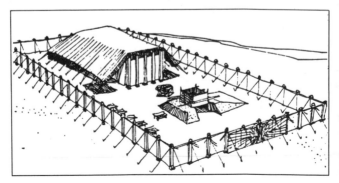

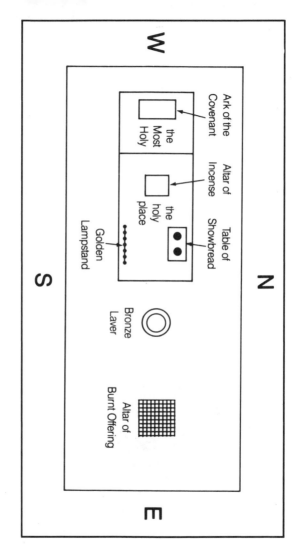

This illustration shows the relative positions of the tabernacle furniture used in Israelite worship. The tabernacle is enlarged for clarity.

The Furniture of the Tabernacle
(Exodus 24–27)

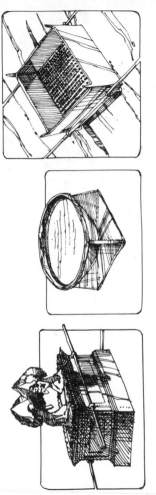

Ark of the Covenant
(Ex. 25:10–22)
The ark was most sacred of all the furniture in the tabernacle. Here the Hebrews kept a copy of the Ten Commandments, which summarized the whole covenant.

Bronze Laver
(Ex. 30:17–21)
It was to the laver of bronze that the priests would come for cleansing. They must be pure to enter the presence of God.

Altar of Burnt Offering
(Ex. 27:1–8)
Animal sacrifices were offered on this altar, located in the court in front of the tabernacle. The blood of the sacrifice was sprinkled on the four horns of the altar.

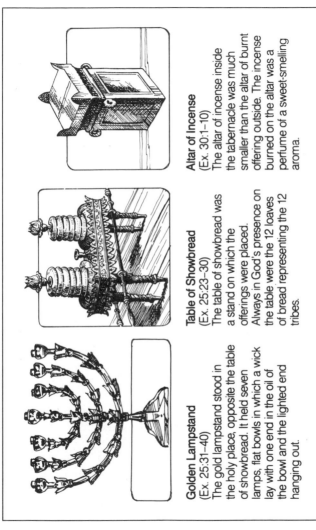

Golden Lampstand
(Ex. 25:31–40)
The gold lampstand stood in the holy place, opposite the table of showbread. It held seven lamps, flat bowls in which a wick lay with one end in the oil of the bowl and the lighted end hanging out.

Table of Showbread
(Ex. 25:23–30)
The table of showbread was a stand on which the offerings were placed. Always in God's presence on the table were the 12 loaves of bread representing the 12 tribes.

Altar of Incense
(Ex. 30:1–10)
The altar of incense inside the tabernacle was much smaller than the altar of burnt offering outside. The incense burned on the altar was a perfume of a sweet-smelling aroma.

Chronology of Israel in the Pentateuch

This chart summarizes biblical information on some key events and movements of Israel in Exodus through Deuteronomy.

Date	Event	Reference
Fifteenth day, first month, first year	Exodus	Ex. 12
Fifteenth day, second month, first year	Arrival in Wilderness of Sin	Ex. 16:1
Third month, first year	Arrival in Wilderness of Sinai	Ex. 19:1
First day, first month, second year	Erection of Tabernacle Dedication of Altar Consecration of Levites	Ex. 40:17 Num. 7:1 Num. 8:1–26
Fourteenth day, first month, second year	Passover	Num. 9:5
First day, second month, second year	Census	Num. 1:1, 18
Fourteenth day, second month, second year	Supplemental Passover	Num. 9:11
Twentieth day, second month, second year	Departure from Sinai	Num. 10:11

First month, fortieth year	In Wilderness of Zin	Num. 20:1, 22–29; 33:38
First day, fifth month, fortieth year	Death of Aaron	Num. 20:22–29; 33:38
First day, eleventh month, fortieth year	Moses' Address	Deut. 1:3

The Book of
LEVITICUS

◆

LANDMARKS OF LEVITICUS

Key Word: *Holiness*

Leviticus centers around the concept of the holiness of God, and how an unholy people can acceptably approach Him and then remain in continued fellowship.

Key Verses: *Leviticus 17:11; 20:7, 8*

Key Chapter: *Leviticus 16*

The Day of Atonement (*"Yom Kippur"*) was the most important single day in the Hebrew calendar as it was the only day the high priests entered into the Holy of Holies to "make atonement for you, to cleanse you, *that* you may be clean from all your sins before the LORD" (16:30).

◆

Overview of Leviticus

FOCUS	Sacrifice				Sanctification				
REFERENCE	1:1 —— 8:1	—— 11:1	—— 16:1	—— 18:1	—— 21:1	—— 23:1	—— 25:1	—— 27:1	—— 27:34
DIVISION	The Laws of Sacrifice				The Laws of Sanctification				
DIVISION	The Offerings	Consecration of the Priests	Consecration of the People	National Atonement	For the People	For the Priests	In Worship	In the Land of Canaan	Through Vows
TOPIC	The Way to God				The Walk with God				
TOPIC	The Laws of Acceptable Approach to God				The Laws of Continued Fellowship with God				
LOCATION	Mount Sinai								
TIME	c. 1 Month								

Ceremonial Laws
(Leviticus 17—26)

The concept of ceremonial holiness in Leviticus springs from the truths that God is holy, and only persons ritually clean can approach Him in worship: "For I *am* the LORD your God. You shall therefore sanctify yourselves, and you shall be holy; for I *am* holy" (Lev. 11:44). Chapters 17—26 of Leviticus are known as the "Holiness Code," but the books of Numbers and Deuteronomy also contain many related regulations.

While this ceremonial system served a valuable purpose for God's people in Old Testament times, the sacrifice of Christ, the great High Priest, has removed the need for ceremonial regulations while stressing the moral law.

The Levitical Offerings
(Leviticus 1—7)

1. Burnt Offering (*olah,* Heb.)
Sweet aroma; Voluntary. Lev. 1:3–17; 6:8–13.

Purpose: (1) To propitiate for sin in general (1:4). (2) To signify complete dedication and consecration to God; hence it is called the "whole burnt offering."

Consisted of: According to wealth: (1) Bull without blemish (1:3–9); (2) Male sheep or goat without blemish (1:10–13); (3) Turtledoves or young pigeons (1:14–17).

God's Portion: Entirety burned on the altar of burnt offering (1:9), except the skin (7:8).

Priests' Portion: Skin only (7:8).

Prophetic Significance Signifies complete dedication of life to God: (1) On the part of Christ (Matt. 26:39–44; Mark 14:36; Luke 22:42; Phil. 2:5–11). (2) On the part of the believer (Rom. 12:1–2; Heb. 13:15).

2. Grain Offering (*minhah,* Heb.)
Sweet aroma; Voluntary. Lev. 2:1–16; 6:14–18; 7:12, 13.

Purpose: The grain offering accompanied all the burnt offerings; it signified one's homage and thanksgiving to God.

Consisted of: Three types: (1) Fine flour mixed with oil and frankincense (2:1–3); (2) Cakes made of fine flour mixed with oil and baked in an oven (2:4), in a pan (2:5), or in a covered pan (2:7); (3) Green heads of roasted grain mixed with oil and frankincense (2:14, 15).

God's Portion: Memorial portion burned on the altar of burnt offering (2:2, 9, 16).

Priests' Portion: Remainder to be eaten in the court of the tabernacle (2:3, 10; 6:16–18; 7:14, 15).

Prophetic Significance: Signifies the perfect humanity of Christ: (1) The absence of leaven typifies the sinlessness of Christ (Heb. 4:15; 1 John 3:5). (2) The presence of oil is emblematic of the Holy Spirit (Luke 4:18; 1 John 2:20, 27).

3. Peace Offering (*shelem,* Heb.)
Sweet aroma; Voluntary. Lev. 3:1–17; 7:11–21, 28–34.

Purpose: The peace offering generally expressed peace and fellowship between the offerer and God; hence it culmi-

nated in a communal meal. There were three types:
(1) Thank Offering—to express gratitude for an unexpected blessing or deliverance. (2) Votive Offering—to express gratitude for a blessing or deliverance granted when a vow had accompanied the petition. (3) Freewill Offering—to express gratitude to God without regard to any specific blessing or deliverance.

Consisted of: According to wealth: (1) From the herd, a male or female without blemish (3:1–5); (2) From the flock, a male or female without blemish (3:6–11); (3) From the goats (3:12–17).

Note: Minor imperfections were permitted when the peace offering was a freewill offering of a bull or a lamb (22:23).

God's Portion: Fatty portions burned on the altar of burnt offering (3:3–5).

Priests' Portion: Breast (wave offering) and right thigh (heave offering; 7:30–34).

Offerer's Portion: Remainder to be eaten in the court by the offerer and his family: (1) Thank offering—to be eaten the same day (7:15). (2) Votive and freewill offerings—to be eaten the first and second day (7:16–18).

Note: This is the only offering in which the offerer shared.

Prophetic Significance: Foreshadows the peace which the believer has with God through Jesus Christ (Rom. 5:1; Col. 1:20).

4. Sin Offering (*hattat,* Heb.)
    Non-sweet aroma; Compulsory. Lev. 4:1—5:13;
    6:24–30.

Purpose: To atone for sins committed unknowingly, especially where no restitution was possible. Note Num. 15:30, 31: The sin offering was of no avail in cases of defiant rebellion against God.

Consisted of: (1) For the high priest, a bull without blemish (4:3–12). (2) For the congregation, a bull without blemish (4:13–21). (3) For a ruler, a male goat without blemish (4:22–26). (4) For a commoner, a female goat or female lamb without blemish (4:27–35). (5) In cases of poverty, two turtledoves or two young pigeons (one for a sin offering, the other for a burnt offering) could be substituted (5:7–10). (6) In cases of extreme poverty, fine flour could be substituted (5:11–13; cf. Heb 9:22).

God's Portion: (7) Fatty portions to be burned on the altar of burnt offering (4:8–10, 19, 26, 31, 35). (8) When the sin offering was for the high priest or congregation, the remainder of the bull was to be burned outside the camp (4:11, 12, 20, 21).

Priests' Portion: When the sin offering was for a ruler or commoner, the remainder of the goat or lamb was to be eaten in the tabernacle court (6:26).

Prophetic Significance: Prefigures the fact that in His death: (1) Christ was made sin for us (2 Cor. 5:21); (2) Christ suffered outside the gates of Jerusalem (Heb. 13:11–13).

5. Trespass Offering *('asham,* Heb.)
   Non-sweet aroma; Compulsory. Lev. 5:14—6:7; 7:1–7.

Purpose: To atone for sins commited unknowingly, especially where restitution was possible.

The Jewish Calendar

The Jews used two kinds of calendars:
> *Civil Calendar*—official calendar of kings, childbirth, and contracts.
>
> *Sacred Calendar*—from which festivals were computed.

NAMES OF MONTHS	CORRESPONDS WITH	NO. OF DAYS	MONTH OF CIVIL YEAR	MONTH OF SACRED YEAR
TISHRI	Sept.–Oct.	30 days	1st	7th
HESHVAN	Oct.–Nov.	29 or 30	2nd	8th
CHISLEV	Nov.–Dec.	29 or 30	3rd	9th
TEBETH	Dec.–Jan.	29	4th	10th
SHEBAT	Jan.–Feb.	30	5th	11th
ADAR	Feb.–Mar.	29 or 30	6th	12th
NISAN	Mar.–Apr.	30	7th	1st
IYAR	Apr.–May	29	8th	2nd
SIVAN	May–June	30	9th	3rd
TAMMUZ	June–July	29	10th	4th
AB	July–Aug.	30	11th	5th
*ELUL	Aug.–Sept.	29	12th	6th

The Jewish day was from sunset to sunset, in 8 equal parts:

FIRST WATCH	SUNSET TO 9 P.M.
SECOND WATCH	9 P.M. TO MIDNIGHT
THIRD WATCH	MIDNIGHT TO 3 A.M.
FOURTH WATCH	3 A.M. TO SUNRISE
FIRST HOUR	SUNRISE TO 9 A.M.
THIRD HOUR	9 A.M. TO NOON
SIXTH HOUR	NOON TO 3 P.M.
NINTH HOUR	3 P.M. TO SUNSET

*Hebrew months were alternately 30 and 29 days long. Their year, shorter than ours, had 354 days. Therefore, about every three years (7 times in 19 years) an extra 29-day month, VEADAR, was added between ADAR and NISAN.

Consisted of: (1) If the offense were against the Lord (tithes, offerings, etc.), a ram without blemish was to be brought; restitution was reckoned according to the priest's estimate of the value of the trespass, plus one-fifth (5:15, 16). (2) If the offense were against man, a ram without blemish was to be brought; restitution was reckoned according to the value plus one-fifth (6:4–6).

God's Portion: Fatty portions to be burned on the altar of burnt offering (7:3–5).

Priests' Portion: Remainder to be eaten in a holy place (7:6, 7).

Prophetic Significance: Foreshadows the fact that Christ is also our trespass offering (Col. 2:13).

The Feasts of the Lord

1. **Passover** (*pesah,* Heb.).
   Ex. 12:1–28, 43–49; Lev. 23:5; Num. 28:16; Deut. 16:1–8

Time: The evening of the fourteenth day of Nisan (Abib), the first month of the biblical year (March/April).

Purpose: (1) To commemorate Israel's deliverance from Egyptian bondage. (2) To remind the children of Israel that God "passed over" their houses, i.e., spared the firstborn of the Israelites (Ex. 12:27).

Prophetic Significance: (1) Christ is our Passover (cf. John 1:29; 19:36; 1 Cor. 5:7; 1 Pet. 1:18, 19). (2) The Passover is the foundation for the Lord's Supper (cf. Matt. 26:17–30; Mark 14:12–25; Luke 22:1–20). (3) The Passover foreshadows the marriage supper of the Lamb (cf. Matt. 26:29; Mark 14:25; Luke 22:16–18).

2. Feast of Unleavened Bread (*matsot,* Heb.).
Ex. 12:15–20; 13:3–10; Lev. 23:6–8; Num. 28:17–25; Deut. 16:3–8

Time: It began on the fifteenth day of Nisan (Abib) and continued for one week (March/April).

Purpose: To commemorate the hardships of Israel's hurried flight from Egypt (Ex. 12:39). The absence of leaven symbolized complete consecration and devotion to God.

Prophetic Significance: (1) Unleavened bread is a type of Christ (cf. John 6:30–59; 1 Cor. 11:24). (2) Unleavened bread is a type of the true church (cf. 1 Cor. 5:7, 8).

3. Day of Firstfruits (*bikkurim,* Heb.).
Lev. 23:9–14

Time: On the day after the Sabbath of Passover week (March/April).

Purpose: To dedicate and consecrate the firstfruits of the barley harvest.

Prophetic Significance: (1) Firstfruits is a type of the bodily resurrection of Christ (cf. 1 Cor. 15:20–23). (2) Firstfruits is a guarantee of the bodily resurrection of all believers (cf. 1 Cor. 15:20–23; 1 Thess. 4:13–18). (3) Firstfruits is a type of the consecration of the church.

4. Feast of Pentecost (or Weeks: *shabuot,* Heb.).
Lev. 23:15–22; Num. 28:26–31; Deut. 16:9–12

Time: The day after the seventh Sabbath after the Day of Firstfruits (May/June).

Purpose: To dedicate and consecrate the firstfruits of the wheat harvest.

Prophetic Significance: The outpouring of the Holy Spirit upon the church occurred on the Day of Pentecost (Acts 2). The two loaves, representative of the Jew and Gentile, contained leaven because sin is found within the church.

5. Day of Trumpets (*rosh hashanah,* Heb.).
Lev. 23:23–25; Num. 10:10; 29:1–6

Time: The first day of the seventh month (Tishri), the sabbatical month (September/October).

Purpose: To usher in and consecrate the seventh month as the sabbatical month.

Prophetic Significance: In the N.T. the blowing of the trumpet is associated with the return of our Lord (cf. Matt. 24:31; 1 Cor. 15:52; 1 Thess. 4:16).

6. Day of Atonement (*yom kippur,* Heb.).
Lev. 16; 23:26–32; Num. 29:7–11

Time: The tenth day of the seventh month (Tishri—September/October).

Purpose: To make annual atonement for the sins of the priests and the people, and for the tabernacle (temple).

Prophetic Significance: The Day of Atonement finds its ultimate fulfillment in the crucifixion of Christ (cf. Heb. 9). It represents the redeeming work of Christ more adequately than any other O.T. type.

7. **Feast of Tabernacles** (Booths or Ingathering; *sukkot,*
   Heb.).
   Lev. 23:33–43; Num. 29:12–38; Deut. 16:13–17

Time: The fifteenth through twenty-first of the seventh
month (Tishri), with an eighth day added as a climax to all
the feasts (September/October).

Purpose: (1) To commemorate God's deliverance and protection during the wilderness wanderings (23:43).
(2) To rejoice in the completion of all the harvest (23:39).

Prophetic Significance: The Feast of Tabernacles foreshadows the peace and prosperity of the millennial reign
of Christ (Zech. 14:16).

Israel's Other Sacred Times

Besides the Annual Feasts, Israel's time was marked by
these other sacred events.

Sabbath

Every seventh day was a solemn rest from all work (Ex.
20:8–11; 31:12–17; Lev. 23:3; Deut. 5:12–15).

Sabbath Year

Every seventh year was designated a ''year of release'' to
allow the land to lie fallow (Ex. 23:10, 11; Lev. 25:1–7).

Year of Jubilee

The 50th year, which followed seven Sabbath years, was
to proclaim liberty to those who were servants because of
debt, and to return lands to their former owners (Lev.
25:8–55; 27:17–24; Ezek. 46:17).

The New Moon

The first day of the Hebrew 29- or 30-day month was a day of rest, special sacrifices, and the blowing of trumpets (Num. 28:11–15; Ps. 81:3).

Dedication (Lights or *Hanukkah*)

An eight-day feast in the ninth month (Chislev) commemorating the cleansing of the temple from defilement by Syria, and its rededication (John 10:22).

Purim (Lots)

A feast on the 14th and 15th of the 12th month (Adar). The name comes from Babylonian *Pur,* meaning ''Lot'' (Esth. 9:18–32).

The Book of
NUMBERS

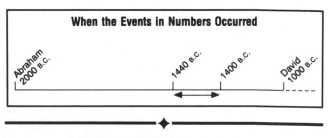

When the Events in Numbers Occurred

Abraham 2000 B.C. — 1440 B.C. — 1400 B.C. — David 1000 B.C.

LANDMARKS OF NUMBERS

Key Word: *Wanderings*

Numbers records the failure of Israel to believe in the promise of God and the resulting judgment of wandering in the wilderness for forty years.

Key Verses: *Numbers 14:22, 23; 20:12*

Key Chapter: *Numbers 14*

The critical turning point of Numbers may be seen in Numbers 14 when Israel rejects God by refusing to go up and conquer the Promised Land.

---◆---

Placement of Tribes in the Israelite Encampment
(Numbers 2)

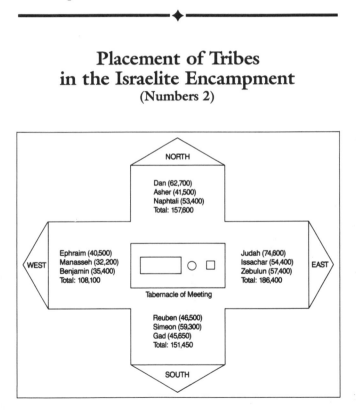

NORTH

Dan (62,700)
Asher (41,500)
Naphtali (53,400)
Total: 157,600

WEST

Ephraim (40,500)
Manasseh (32,200)
Benjamin (35,400)
Total: 108,100

EAST

Judah (74,600)
Issachar (54,400)
Zebulun (57,400)
Total: 186,400

Tabernacle of Meeting

Reuben (46,500)
Simeon (59,300)
Gad (45,650)
Total: 151,450

SOUTH

Overview of Numbers

FOCUS	The Old Generation		The Tragic Transition				The New Generation		
REFERENCE	1:1 ———	5:1 ———	10:11 —	13:1 —	15:1 ———	20:1 —	26:1 ———	28:1 ———	31:1 ———36:13
DIVISION	Organization of Israel	Sanctification of Israel	To Kadesh	At Kadesh	In Wilderness	To Moab	Reorganization of Israel	Regulations of Offerings and Vows	Conquest and Division of Israel
TOPIC	Order		Disorder				Reorder		
TOPIC	Preparation		Postponement				Preparation		
LOCATION	Mount Sinai		Wilderness				Plains of Moab		
TIME	20 Days		30 Years 3 Months and 10 Days				c. 5 Months		

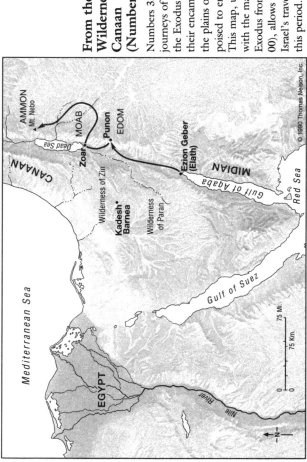

From the Wilderness to Canaan (Numbers 33)

Numbers 33 reviews the journeys of Israel from the Exodus through their encampment on the plains of Moab, poised to enter Canaan. This map, used along with the map "The Exodus from Egypt" (p. 00), allows you to trace Israel's travels during this period.

© 1990 Thomas Nelson, Inc.

Mediterranean Sea

EGYPT

Nile River

Gulf of Suez

Gulf of Aqaba

Red Sea

CANAAN

Dead Sea

Zoar

MOAB

Mt. Nebo

AMMON

Punon

EDOM

Wilderness of Zin

Kadesh Barnea

Wilderness of Paran

Ezion Geber (Elath)

MIDIAN

75 Mi.

75 Km.

N

Overview of Deuteronomy

FOCUS	First Sermon	Second Sermon				Third Sermon		
REFERENCE	1:1 ——— 4:44 ———	12:1 ———		16:18 — 21:1 —	27:1 ———	29:1 ———	31:1 ———	34:12
DIVISION	Review of God's Acts for Israel	Exposition of the Decalogue	Ceremonial Laws	Civil Laws	Social Laws	Ratification of Covenant	Palestinian Covenant	Transition of Covenant Mediator
TOPIC	What God Has Done	What God Expected of Israel				What God Will Do		
	Historical	Legal				Prophetical		
LOCATION	Plains of Moab							
TIME	c. 1 Month							

The Book of
DEUTERONOMY

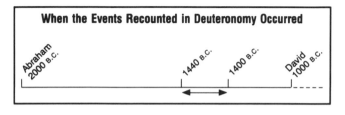

When the Events Recounted in Deuteronomy Occurred

Abraham 2000 B.C. — 1440 B.C. — 1400 B.C. — David 1000 B.C.

LANDMARKS OF DEUTERONOMY

Key Word: *Covenant*

The primary theme of the entire Book of Deuteronomy is the renewal of the covenant.

Key Verses: *Deuteronomy 10:12, 13; 30:19, 20*

Key Chapter: *Deuteronomy 27*

The formal ratification of the covenant occurs in Deuteronomy 27, as Moses, the priests, the Levites, and all of Israel "take heed and listen, O Israel: This day you have become the people of the LORD your God" (27:9).

Deuteronomy as a Treaty

Meredith Kline maintains that the whole Book of Deuteronomy, plus the Ten Commandments and passages such as Joshua 24, are written in the form of an ancient covenant, or treaty, between a monarch and his subjects. In this case the Monarch was God and His subjects were the Israelites. Kline details five parts in his *Treaty to the Great King*. Whether or not Deuteronomy was actually designed on this pattern, material very similar to these parts occurs in Deuteronomy:

1. Preamble, identifying the suzerain, or lord (Deut. 1:1–5).
2. Prologue, describing previous history of relationships (Deut. 1:6—3:29).
3. Stipulations and demands of the suzerain (Deut. 4—26).
4. Ratifications, or swearing allegiance, with benefits for keeping the treaty and curses for breaking it (Deut. 27—30).
5. Witnesses and instructions for implementing the covenant (Deut. 31—34).

Crimes Allowing the Death Penalty

Crime	Scripture Reference
1. Premeditated Murder—Death Penalty Required	Ex. 21:12–14, 22, 23
2. Kidnapping	Ex. 21:16; Deut. 24:7
3. Striking or Cursing Parents	Ex. 21:15; Lev. 20:9; Prov. 20:20; Matt. 15:4; Mark 7:10
4. Magic and Divination	Ex. 22:18
5. Bestiality	Ex. 22:19; Lev. 20:15, 16
6. Sacrificing to False Gods	Ex. 22:20
7. Profaning the Sabbath	Ex. 35:2; Num. 15:32–36
8. Offering Human Sacrifice	Lev. 20:2

9. Adultery	Lev. 20:10–21; Deut. 22:22
10. Incest	Lev. 20:11, 12, 14
11. Homosexuality	Lev. 20:13
12. Blasphemy	Lev. 24:11–14, 16, 23
13. False Prophecy	Deut. 13:1–10
14. Incorrigible Rebelliousness	Deut. 17:12; 21:18–21
15. Fornication	Deut. 22:20, 21
16. Rape of Betrothed Virgin	Deut. 22:23–27

Cities of Refuge

Six cities of refuge were designed throughout Israel in Old Testament times to provide a haven for people who killed other persons by accident. Protection like this was necessary because of the "avenger of blood," the relative who considered it his duty to slay the killer. Eligibility for refuge was determined by a judge. For convenience, three of the cities were located on either side of the Jordan River.

Bezer: Located in the wilderness plateau of Moab, Bezer was a walled city within the territory of Reuben (Deut. 4:43).

Golan: Located in the area known as Bashan, Golan was 17 miles east of the Sea of Galilee. This general area today is often called the Golan Heights (Deut. 4:43).

Hebron: The southernmost of the six cities, Hebron was 20 miles south of Jerusalem. It was also known as Kirjath Arba (Josh. 20:7).

Kedesh: Also known as Kedesh Naphtali, this city was located in Galilee in the mountains of Naphtali (Josh. 20:7).

Ramoth: Also known as Ramoth Gilead, Ramoth was an important walled city in the territory of Gad. It was located about 25 miles east of the Jordan River near the border of Syria (Deut. 4:43).

Shechem: Located in the mountains of Ephraim, this is the city where the Lord appeared to Abraham with the promise, "To your descendants I will give this land" (Gen. 12:6, 7).

Hymns and Songs

The earliest recorded song in the Bible is referred to as the Song of Moses (see Ex. 15). This hymn was sung by the people to celebrate God's miraculous deliverance of the Hebrews from the Egyptian army at the Red Sea (Ex. 14:3–30), and Moses sang again just before his death. Other significant hymns and songs in the Old Testament include the following:

Personality	Description	Biblical Reference
Israelites	Sung by the people as they dug life-saving wells in the Wilderness	Num. 21:14–18
Moses	A song of praise to God by Moses just before his death	Deut. 32:1–44
Deborah and Barak	A victory song after Israel's defeat of the Canaanites	Judg. 5:1–31
Israelite Women	A song to celebrate David's defeat of Goliath	1 Sam. 18:6, 7
Levite Singers	A song of praise at the dedication of the temple in Jerusalem	2 Chr. 5:12–14

| Levite Singers | A song of praise, presented as a marching song as the army of Israel prepared for battle | 2 Chr. 20:20–23 |
| Levite Singers | A song at the temple restoration ceremony during Hezekiah's reign | 2 Chr. 29:25–30 |

Mountains of the Bible

Mountains are a location where God has met with His people throughout the Scripture. God gave Moses the Law atop Mt. Sinai, and Moses commanded that an altar be built atop Mt. Ebal when the Israelites entered the Promised Land. Although God did not permit Moses to enter that long-awaited land, He did allow him to view it from Mt. Pisgah. God buried Moses there on the mountain with His own hands. Following are several significant mountains of the Scriptures:

Mt. Ararat: Ararat (in modern Turkey), where Noah's ark came to rest (Gen. 8:4).

Mt. Carmel: Carmel, where Elijah was victorious over the prophets of Baal (1 Kin. 18:9–42).

Mt. Ebal: Ebal (opposite Mt. Gerizim), where Moses commanded that an altar be built after the Hebrews entered the Promised Land.

Mt. Gerizim: Gerizim, where Jesus talked with the Samaritan woman at the well (John 4:20).

Mt. Gilboa: Gilboa, where King Saul and his sons were killed in a battle with the Philistines (1 Chr. 10:1, 8).

Mt. Hermon: Hermon, a mountain range that marked the northern limit of the conquest of Canaan (Josh. 11:3, 17).

Mt. Lebanon: Lebanon, source of cedar wood for Solomon's temple in Jerusalem (1 Kings 5:14, 18).

Mt. Olivet: Olivet, or Mt. of Olives, where Jesus gave the discourse on His Second Coming (Matt. 24:3).

Mt. Pisgah: Pisgah, or Nebo, where Moses viewed the Promised Land.

Mt. Sinai: Sinai, or Horeb (near Egypt), where the law was given to Moses (Ex. 19:2–25).

TWO

BOOKS OF HISTORY

♦

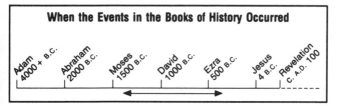

The Book of JOSHUA

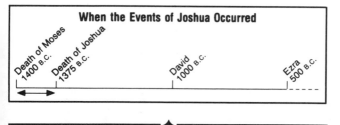

♦

LANDMARKS OF JOSHUA

Key Word: *Conquest*

The entire Book of Joshua describes the entering, conquering, and occupying of the land of Canaan.

Overview of Joshua

FOCUS	Conquest of Canaan		Settlement in Canaan			
REFERENCE	1:1 ——— 6:1	——— 13:8	——— 14:1	——— 20:1	——— 22:1	——— 24:33
DIVISION	Preparation of Israel	Conquest of Canaan	Settlement of East Jordan	Settlement of West Jordan	Settlement of Religious Community	Conditions for Continued Settlement
TOPIC	Entering Canaan	Conquering Canaan	Dividing Canaan			
	Preparation	Subjection	Possession			
LOCATION	Jordan River	Canaan	Two and a Half Tribes—East Jordan / Nine and a Half Tribes—West Jordan			
TIME	c. 1 Month	c. 7 Years	c. 8 Years			

Key Verses: *Joshua 1:8; 11:23*

Key Chapter: *Joshua 24*

Joshua reviews for the people God's fulfillment of His promises and then challenges them to review their commitment to the covenant (24:24, 25), which is the foundation for all successful national life.

---◆---

The Conquest of Canaan
(Joshua 6—13)

Central and Southern Campaigns
(Joshua 6—10)

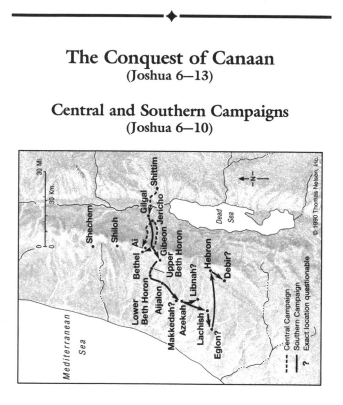

The Conquest of Canaan
(Joshua 6—13)

Northern Campaign
(Joshua 11)

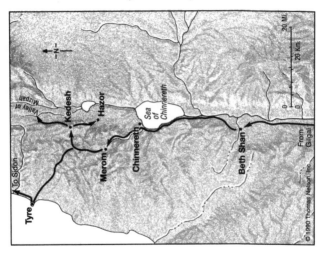

Victory and Settlement

The central, southern, and northern campaigns under Joshua are described briefly in chapters 1—11 and probably covered a period of about seven years around 1400 B.C. By the time Joshua died (Josh. 24:29), the Israelites had driven most of the Canaanites out of Palestine and divided the land among the twelve tribes of Israel (see map p. 57). The tribe of Levi had no land; they were set apart for God's service and this was their inheritance.

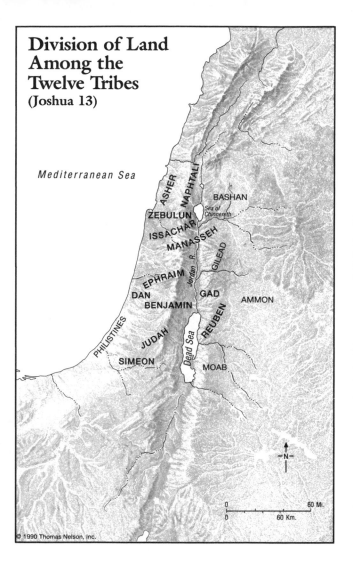

Division of Land Among the Twelve Tribes
(Joshua 13)

Mediterranean Sea

ASHER

NAPHTALI

BASHAN

ZEBULUN

Sea of
Chinnereth

ISSACHAR

MANASSEH

GILEAD

EPHRAIM

Jordan R.

DAN

GAD

AMMON

BENJAMIN

PHILISTINES

REUBEN

JUDAH

Dead Sea

SIMEON

MOAB

—N—

0   60 Mi.

0   60 Km.

© 1990 Thomas Nelson, Inc.

Overview of Judges

FOCUS	Deterioration		Deliverance						Depravity		
REFERENCE	1:1 ——	2:1 —— 3:5 ——	4:1 ——	6:1 ——	10:6 ——	12:8 ——	13:1 ——	17:1 ——	19:1 ——	20:1–21:25	
DIVISION	Israel Fails to Complete Conquest	God Judges Israel	Southern Campaign	Northern Campaign (1st)	Central Campaign	Eastern Campaign	Northern Campaign (2nd)	Western Campaign	Sin of Idolatry	Sin of Immorality	Sin of Civil War
TOPIC	Causes of the Cycles		Curse of the Cycles						Conditions During the Cycles		
	Living with the Canaanites		War with the Canaanites						Living Like the Canaanites		
LOCATION	Canaan										
TIME	c. 350 Years										

The Book of
JUDGES

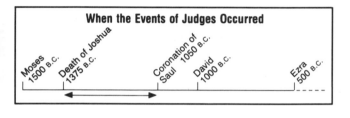

When the Events of Judges Occurred

Moses 1500 B.C. — Death of Joshua 1375 B.C. — Coronation of Saul 1050 B.C. — David 1000 B.C. — Ezra 500 B.C.

◆

LANDMARKS OF JUDGES

Key Word: *Cycles*

The Book of Judges is written primarily on a thematic rather than a chronological basis (16—21 actually precede 3—15). The author uses the accounts of the various judges to prove the utter failure of living out the closing verse of Judges: "Everyone did *what was* right in his own eyes." To accomplish this, the author uses a five-point cycle to recount the repeated spiral of disobedience, destruction, and defeat. The five parts are: (1) sin, (2) servitude, (3) supplication, (4) salvation, and (5) silence.

Key Verses: *Judges 2:20, 21; 21:25*

Key Chapter: *Judges 2*

The second chapter of Judges is a miniature of the whole book as it records the transition of the godly to the ungodly generation, the format of the cycles, and the purpose of God in not destroying the Canaanites.

◆

The Path of Gideon

One of the most notable deliverers called by God during the dark period of the Judges was Gideon (6:11—8:32). An angel of the Lord appeared to him at Ophrah, but Gideon "put out the fleece" twice for a sign before he went to battle. Gideon's military victories under the guidance of the Lord were great, but near the end of his life he made a golden ephod which led the people into idolatry.

Gideon's Campaign
(Judges 6:11—8:32)

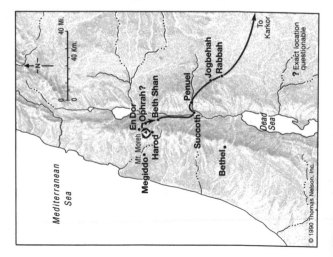

The Judges of Israel

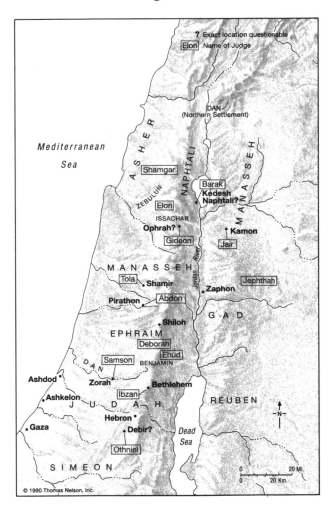

Mediterranean Sea

? Exact location questionable

Elon Name of Judge

DAN (Northern Settlement)

ASHER

ZEBULUN

NAPHTALI

MANASSEH

Shamgar

Barak
Kedesh
Naphtali?

Elon

ISSACHAR

Ophrah?

Gideon

Kamon

Jair

MANASSEH

Jordan River

Tola

Shamir

Zaphon

Jephthah

Pirathon

Abdon

GAD

Shiloh

EPHRAIM

Deborah

Ehud

Samson

BENJAMIN

Ashdod

Zorah

Ibzan

Bethlehem

Ashkelon

DAN

REUBEN

JUDAH

Gaza

Hebron

Debir?

Dead Sea

Othniel

SIMEON

0   20 Mi.
0   20 Km.

-N-

© 1990 Thomas Nelson, Inc.

The Period of the Judges

Judge and Tribe	Scripture References	Oppressors	Period of Oppression/Rest
(1) **Othniel** (Judah) Son of Kenaz, younger brother of Caleb	Judg. 1:11–15; 3:1–11 Josh. 15:16–19; 1 Chr. 4:13	Cushan-Rishathaim, king of Mesopotamia	8 years/40 years
(2) **Ehud** (Benjamin) Son of Gera	Judg. 3:12–4:1	Eglon, king of Moab; Ammonites; Amalekites	18 years/80 years
(3) **Shamgar** (Perhaps foreign) Son of Anath	Judg. 3:31; 5:6	Philistines	Not given/Not given
(4) **Deborah** (Ephraim), **Barak** (Naphtali) Son of Abinoam	Judg. 4:1–5:31 Heb. 11:32	Jabin, king of Canaan; Sisera commander of army	20 years/40 years
(5) **Gideon** (Manasseh) Son of Joash the Abiezrite. Also called: Jerubbaal (6:32; 7:1); Jerubbesheth (2 Sam. 11:21)	Judg. 6:1–8:32 Heb. 11:32	Midianites; Amalekites; "People of the East"	7 years/40 years

(6) **Abimelech** (Manasseh) Son of Gideon by a concubine	Judg. 8:33—9:57 2 Sam. 11:21	Civil war	Abimelech ruled over Israel 3 years
(7) **Tola** (Issachar) Son of Puah	Judg. 10:1, 2		Judged Israel 23 years
(8) **Jair** (Gilead-Manasseh)	Judg. 10:3–5		Judged Israel 22 years
(9) **Jephthah** (Gilead-Manasseh) Son of Gilead by a harlot	Judg. 10:6—12:7 Heb. 11:32	Philistines; Ammonites; Civil war with the Ephramites	18 years/Judged Israel 6 years
(10) **Ibzan** (Judah or Zebulun) (Bethlehem-Zebulun; cf. Josh. 19:15)	Judg. 12:8–10		Judged Israel 7 years
(11) **Elon** (Zebulun)	Judg. 12:11, 12		Judged Israel 10 years
(12) **Abdon** (Ephraim) Son of Hillel	Judg. 12:13–15		Judged Israel 8 years
(13) **Samson** (Dan) Son of Manoah	Judg. 13:1—16:31 Heb. 11:32	Philistines	40 years/Judged Israel 20 years

Overview of Ruth

FOCUS	Ruth's Love Demonstrated			Ruth's Love Rewarded	
REFERENCE	1:1 ——— 1:19 ———		3:1 ———	4:1 ——— 4:22	
DIVISION	Ruth's Decision to Stay with Naomi	Ruth's Devotion to Care for Naomi	Ruth's Request for Redemption by Boaz	Ruth's Reward of Redemption by Boaz	
TOPIC	Ruth and Naomi		Ruth and Boaz		
	Death of Family	Ruth Cares for Naomi	Boaz Cares for Ruth	Birth of Family	
LOCATION	Moab	Fields of Bethlehem	Threshing Floor of Bethlehem	Bethlehem	
TIME	c. 12 Years				

The Book of
RUTH

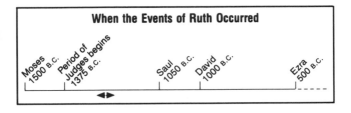

When the Events of Ruth Occurred

Moses 1500 B.C. — Period of Judges begins 1375 B.C. — Saul 1050 B.C. — David 1000 B.C. — Ezra 500 B.C.

◆

LANDMARKS OF RUTH

Key Word: *Kinsman-Redeemer*

The Hebrew word for kinsman *(goel)* appears thirteen times in Ruth and basically means "one who redeems."

Key Verses: *Ruth 1:16; 3:11*

Key Chapter: *Ruth 4*

In twenty-two short verses, Ruth moves from widowhood and poverty to marriage and wealth (2:1). As kinsman-redeemer, Boaz brings a Moabite woman into the family line of David and eventually of Jesus Christ.

◆

The Kinsman-Redeemer

The Book of Ruth portrays both the romantic love story of Ruth the Gentile and Boaz the Jew and the mag-

Moab to Bethlehem—
The Story of Ruth

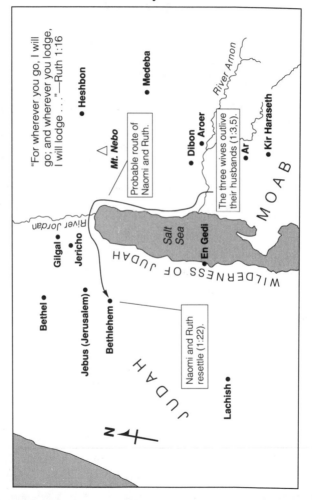

nificent drama of reconciliation between God and humanity. As the kinsman-redeemer Boaz redeemed Ruth from poverty and childlessness, so God redeems helpless and sinful humanity. The qualifications for such a kinsman-redeemer are outlined below.

Kinsman-Redeemer

O.T. Qualification	Christ's Fulfillment
1. Blood Relationship	Gal. 4:4, 5; Heb. 2:16, 17
2. Necessary Resources	1 Cor. 6:20; 1 Pet. 1:18, 19
3. Willingness to Buy	John 10:15–18; 1 John 3:16
4. Willingness to Marry	Rom. 7:4; 2 Cor. 11:2; Eph. 5:25–32; Rev. 19:7

The Book of
FIRST SAMUEL

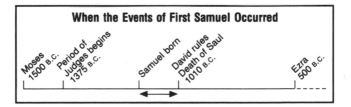

When the Events of First Samuel Occurred

Moses 1500 B.C. — Period of Judges begins 1375 B.C. — Samuel born — David rules Death of Saul 1010 B.C. — Ezra 500 B.C.

Overview of First Samuel

FOCUS	Samuel			Saul		
REFERENCE	1:1 ————	4:1 ————	8:1 ————	13:1 ————	15:10 ————	31:13
DIVISION	First Transition of Leadership Eli–Samuel	Judgeship of Samuel	Second Transition of Leadership Samuel–Saul	Reign of Saul	Third Transition of Leadership Saul–David	
TOPIC	Decline of Judges			Rise of Kings		
	Eli	Samuel		Saul	David	
LOCATION	Canaan					
TIME	c. 94 Years					

LANDMARKS OF FIRST SAMUEL

Key Word: *Transition*

First Samuel records the critical transition in Israel from the rule of God through the judges to His rule through the kings.

Key Verses: *First Samuel 13:14; 15:22*

Key Chapter: *First Samuel 15*

First Samuel 15 records the tragic transition of kingship from Saul to David.

The Life and Ministry of Samuel
(See map next page.)

1. Hannah's prayer at Shiloh was for a son, whom she dedicated to God (1 Sam. 1:10–17).
2. Samuel, son of Elkanah and Hannah, was born at Ramah (1 Sam. 1:20).
3. While Samuel ministered under Eli at Shiloh, God called him to special service (1 Sam. 3:2–21).
4. Every year, Samuel traveled to Bethel, Gilgal, and Mizpeh, as a judge of Israel.
5. Samuel secretly anointed Saul as the first king of Israel in the town of Zuph (1 Sam. 9:5, 6, 27; 10:1).
6. Samuel secretly anointed David as the second king of Israel in Beth-lehem (1 Sam. 16:1, 13).
7. Samuel died and was buried in his hometown of Ramah (1 Sam. 25:1).

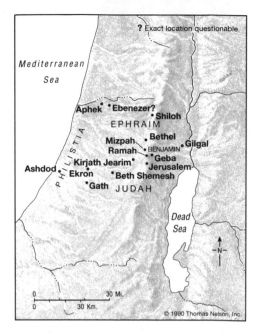

Map labels: ? Exact location questionable; Mediterranean Sea; Aphek; Ebenezer?; Shiloh; EPHRAIM; Mizpah; Bethel; Gilgal; Ramah; BENJAMIN; Kirjath Jearim; Geba; Jerusalem; Ashdod; Ekron; Beth Shemesh; Gath; JUDAH; PHILISTIA; Dead Sea; N; 0 30 Mi.; 0 30 Km.; © 1990 Thomas Nelson, Inc.

Before David Became King
(1 Samuel)

Even as Saul began to fail in his obedience to the Law and commitment to the will of God (see chart p. 72), God sent Samuel to Bethlehem to anoint His choice for a king, the shepherd boy David (ch. 16). Near Sochoh David was welcomed by Saul and defeated the giant Goliath. But once Saul's wrath was kindled against the shepherd soldier, David fled Saul's presence and journeyed to Adullam. Taking his family to the safety of Moab, he established camp at the stronghold (22:4), now known as Masada. From there his activity took him north to Aphek and south to Amalek.

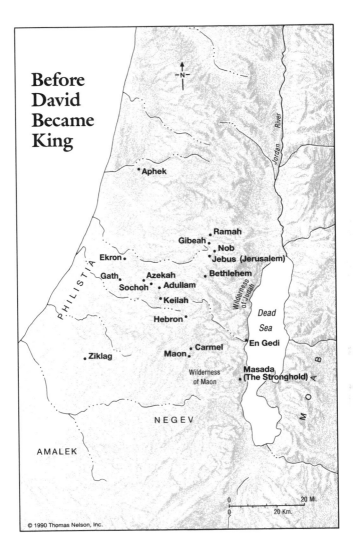

Before David Became King

Aphek

Ramah
Gibeah
Nob
Ekron
Jebus (Jerusalem)
Gath
Azekah
Bethlehem
Sochoh
Adullam
Keilah
Hebron

PHILISTIA

Wilderness of Judah

Dead
Sea

Maon
Carmel
En Gedi

Ziklag

Wilderness
of Maon

Masada
(The Stronghold)

Jordan River

M
O
A
B

NEGEV

AMALEK

0   20 Mi.
0   20 Km.

© 1990 Thomas Nelson, Inc.

King Saul's Decline and Fall
(1 Samuel 13—31)

Causes	Results
A presumptuous sacrifice	Loss of kingdom foretold (13:14)
A foolish curse	Curse falls on Jonathan (14:24, 44)
Spared Agag and flocks	Loss of kingdom (15:28)
Lost fellowship with God	Unanswered prayer (28:6)
Visits a medium	Doom predicted (28:19)
Takes his own life	End of dynasty (31:4, 6)

The Book of
SECOND SAMUEL

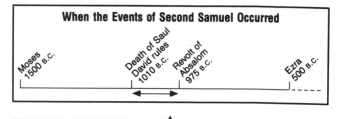

When the Events of Second Samuel Occurred

Moses 1500 B.C.

Death of Saul David rules 1010 B.C.

Revolt of Absalom 975 B.C.

Ezra 500 B.C.

◆

LANDMARKS OF SECOND SAMUEL

Key Word: *David*

The central character of Second Samuel is David, around whom the entire book is written.

Key Verses: *Second Samuel 7:12, 13; 22:21*

Key Chapter: *Second Samuel 11*

The eleventh chapter of 2 Samuel is pivotal for the entire book. This chapter records the tragic sins of David regarding Bathsheba and her husband Uriah. All of the widespread blessings on David's family and his kingdom are quickly removed as God chastises His anointed one.

◆

The Davidic Kingdom
(See map page 75.)

David's military exploits successfully incorporated into the Israelite kingdom the powers of Edom, Moab, Ammon and Zobah. David took the fortress called Jebus and renamed it the "City of David." This established his kingship militarily and politically. He then established his religious leadership by moving the ark of the covenant to the City of David. Solomon later expanded northward to Mt. Moriah and built the temple and the royal palace.

Plot Development of Second Samuel
(See chart page 76.)

The first ten chapters of Second Samuel describe the rewards of obedience as David's rule is extended first over Judah and then over all of Israel. David's crimes of adultery and murder, described in chapter 11, mark the turning point in the book. After this, David's life is a chronicle of trouble and misery—the death of an infant son, incest and murder among David's children, and rebellion against David's kingship.

Second Samuel shows that a person's obedience or disobedience to God has direct consequences for that person's life. But God will rule and overrule so that His long-term purpose of world blessing and redemption may occur.

Overview of Second Samuel

FOCUS	David's Triumphs			David's Transgressions	David's Troubles	
REFERENCE	1:1 ——— 6:1	——— 8:1	——— 11:1	——— 12:1	——— 13:37	——— 24:25
DIVISION	Political Triumphs	Spiritual Triumphs	Military Triumphs	Sins of Adultery and Murder	Troubles in David's House	Troubles in the Kingdom
TOPIC	Success			Sin	Failure	
	Obedience			Disobedience	Judgment	
LOCATION	David in Hebron	David in Jerusalem				
TIME	7½ Years	33 Years				

The Davidic Kingdom
(2 Samuel)

HAMATH

(ZOBAH)

Mediterranean

Sea

PHOENICIA

Damascus

Tyre

Dan

Megiddo

Beth Shan

Shechem

Joppa

ISRAEL

Bethel

Rabbah

Ashdod

Jericho

(AMMON)

Ashkelon

Gath

Jerusalem

PHILISTIA

Dead

Gaza

Hebron

Sea

Raphia

Beersheba

(MOAB)

Zoar

Bozrah

Kadesh Barnea

(EDOM)

—N—

0   60 Mi.

0   60 Km.

© 1990 Thomas Nelson, Inc.

Elath

Plot Development of Second Samuel

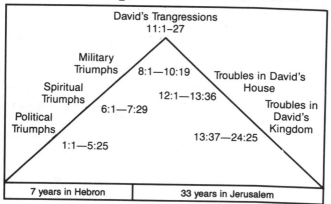

| 7 years in Hebron | 33 years in Jerusalem |

The First Book of KINGS

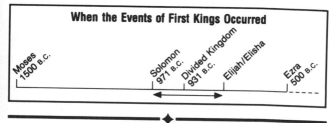

When the Events of First Kings Occurred

Moses 1500 B.C.   Solomon 971 B.C.   Divided Kingdom 931 B.C.   Elijah/Elisha   Ezra 500 B.C.

◆

LANDMARKS OF FIRST KINGS

Key Word: *Division of the Kingdom*

The theme of 1 Kings centers on the fact that the welfare of Israel and Judah depends upon the faithfulness of

Overview of First Kings

FOCUS	United Kingdom			Divided Kingdom			
REFERENCE	1:1 ———	3:1 ———	9:1 ———	12:1 ———	15:1 ———	16:29 ———	22:53
DIVISION	Establishment of Solomon	Rise of Solomon	Decline of Solomon	Division of the Kingdom	Reigns of Various Kings	Reign of Ahab with Elijah	
TOPIC	Solomon			Many Kings			
	Kingdom in Tranquility			Kingdoms in Turmoil			
LOCATION	Jerusalem: Capital of United Kingdom			Samaria: Capital of Israel Jerusalem: Capital of Judah			
TIME	c. 40 Years			c. 90 Years			

the people and their king to the covenant. The two books of Kings trace the monarchy from the point of its greatest prosperity under Solomon to its demise and destruction in the Assyrian and Babylonian captivities. Observance of God's law produces blessing, but apostasy is rewarded by judgment.

Key Verses: *First Kings 9:4, 5; 11:11*

Key Chapter: *First Kings 12*

The critical turning point in 1 Kings occurs in chapter 12, when the united kingdom becomes the divided kingdom upon the death of Solomon.

---◆---

The Kings of Israel and Judah

As the maps on pages 100 and 102 demonstrate, the United Kingdom of Israel reached its peak under King Solomon. Saul, David, and Solomon ruled for 120 years.

After Solomon's death in 930 B.C., his son Rehoboam became king. The ten northern tribes of Israel rebelled and Jeroboam became king of the northern kindom of Israel, with Rehoboam remaining king over the two remaining tribes, now called simply the southern kingdom of Judah (see map p. 100). The chart shows the succession of kings and decline of both kingdoms.

THE UNITED KINGDOM

Saul 1050–1010 B.C.
David 1010–970 B.C.
Solomon 970–930 B.C.

THE DIVIDED KINGDOM

Judah		B.C.	Israel	
		950		
Rehoboam	930–913		Jeroboam I	930–909
		925		
Abijah	913–910		Nadab	909–908
Asa	910–869		Baasha	908–886
		900	Elah	886–885
			Zimri	885
			Tibni	885–880
Jehoshaphat	872–848	875	Omri	885–874
			Ahab	874–853
			Ahaziah	853–852
Jehoram	848–841	850	Joram	852–841
Ahaziah	841		Jehu	841–814
Athaliah	841–835			
Joash	835–796	825		
			Jehoahaz	814–798
Amaziah	796–767	800	Jehoash	798–782
Azariah	792–740		Jeroboam II	793–753
		775		
Jotham	750–735	750	Zechariah	753
			Shallum	752
Ahaz	735–715		Menahem	752–742
		725	Pekahiah	742–740
Hezekiah	715–686		Pekah	752–732
			Hoshea	732–722
Manasseh	697–642	700		
		675		
Amon	642–640	650		
Josiah	640–609	625		
Jehoahaz	609			
Jehoiakim	609–598	600		
Jehoiachin	598–597			
Zedekiah	597–586	586		

Locations in the Ministry of Elijah and Elisha

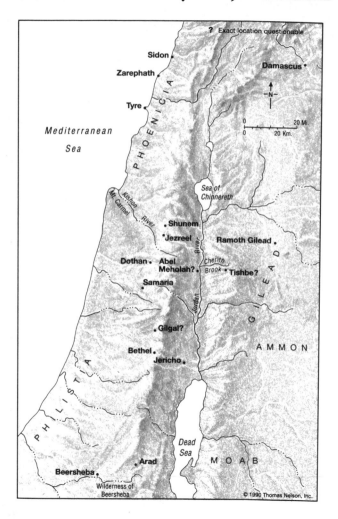

Elijah and Elisha

Elijah's victory on Mt. Carmel ended with the slaying
of 450 prophets of Baal (1 Kin. 18:20–40). His ministry
spanned Canaan from the Brook Cherith near his birthplace (1 Kin. 17:1–7) to Zarephath where he performed the
miracle that sustained the widow and her son, and to as far
south as Mt. Horeb in the Sinai Peninsula. In Samaria Elijah denounced King Ahab's injustice against Naboth of
Jezreel (1 Kin. 21:17–29). Near Jericho Elijah separated the
waters of the Jordan River to cross over and subsequently
was carried to heaven in a chariot of fire (2 Kin. 2:1–12).

Elisha healed Naaman of leprosy in the Jordan River
(2 Kin. 5:1–19) and lead the blinded Syrians to their defeat
at Samaria (2 Kin. 6:8–23). In Damascus, Elisha prophesied the death of King Ben-Hadad of Syria and the succession of Hazael as king of Syria.

Rulers of Syria

Kings	Dates	Scripture References
Hezion (Rezon)	c. 990–730 B.C.	1 Kings 11:23, 25; 15:18
Tabrimmon	c. 930–885 B.C.	1 Kings 15:18
Ben-Hadad I	c. 885–860 B.C.	1 Kings 15:18, 20
Ben-Hadad II	c. 860–841 B.C.	1 Kings 20; 2 Kings 6:24; 8:7, 9, 14
Hazael	c. 841–801 B.C.	1 Kings 19:15, 17; 2 Kings 8; 9:14, 15; 10:32; 12:17, 18; 13:3, 22, 24, 25
Ben-Hadad III	c. 807–780? B.C.	2 Kings 13:3, 24, 25
Rezin	c. 780?–732 B.C.	2 Kings 15:37; 16:5, 6, 9 (cf. Is. 7:1, 4, 8; 8:6; 9:11)

Overview of Second Kings

FOCUS	Divided Kingdom			Surviving Kingdom		
REFERENCE	1:1 ———	9:1 ———	17:1 ———	18:1 ———	22:1 ———	25:1 ——— 25:30
DIVISION	Ministry of Elisha Under Ahaziah and Jehoram	Reigns of Ten Kings of Israel and Eight Kings of Judah	Fall of Israel	Reigns of Hezekiah and Two Evil Kings	Reigns of Josiah and Four Evil Kings	Fall of Judah
TOPIC	Israel and Judah			Judah		
	Ahaziah to Hoshea			Hezekiah to Zedekiah		
LOCATION	Israel Deported to Assyria			Judah Deported to Babylonia		
TIME	131 Years (853–722 B.C.)			155 Years (715–560 B.C.)		

The Second Book of KINGS

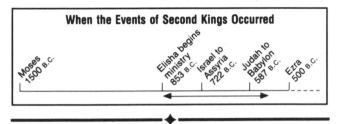

When the Events of Second Kings Occurred

Moses 1500 B.C. — Elisha begins ministry 853 B.C. — Israel to Assyria 722 B.C. — Judah to Babylon 587 B.C. — Ezra 500 B.C.

LANDMARKS OF SECOND KINGS

Key Word: *Captivities of the Kingdom*

Second Kings records both the destruction and captivity of Israel by the Assyrians (2 Kin. 17), as well as the destruction and captivity of Judah by the Babylonians (2 Kin. 25).

The book was written selectively, not exhaustively, from a prophetic viewpoint to teach that the decline and collapse of the two kingdoms occurred because of failure on the part of the rulers and people to heed the warnings of God's messengers.

Key Verses: *Second Kings 17:22, 23; 23:27*

Key Chapter: *Second Kings 25*

The last chapter of 2 Kings records the utter destruction of the city of Jerusalem and its glorious temple. Hope is still alive, however, with the remnant in the Babylonian captivity as Evil-Merodach frees Jehoiachin from prison and treats him kindly.

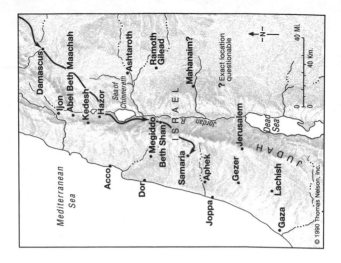

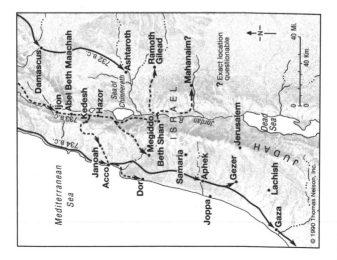

Assyrian Campaigns Against Israel and Judah
(2 Kings 15—18)

From 734 B.C. to 732 B.C. Tiglath-Pileser III mounted one invasion against Judah and two against Israel. (p. 84 top)

In 725 B.C. Shalmanesar V invaded Israel and marched on Samaria. Sargon II took Samaria in 722 B.C. (p. 84 bottom)

Assyrian Campaign Against Judah
(2 Kings 18—19)

Sennacherib moved southward along the coastal plains to Lachish and camped against Jerusalem in 701 B.C.

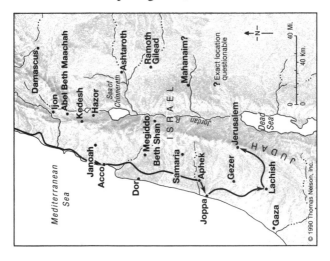

© 1990 Thomas Nelson, Inc.

The Assyrian Empire
(650 B.C.)

This great (and cruel) empire covered the whole of the fertile crescent, with Jerusalem and Judah saved from its complete control by a miraculous defeat of its threatening army (2 Kings 19).

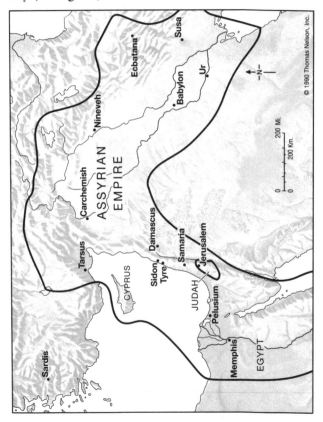

Kings of Assyria

Assur-nasirpal II, 883–859 B.C.   Tiglath-Pileser III, 745–727 B.C.

Shalmaneser III, 858–824 B.C.   Shalmaneser V, 727–722 B.C.

Shamshi-Adad V, 823–811 B.C.   Sargon II, 722–705 B.C.

Adad-nirari III, 810–783 B.C.   Sennacherib, 705–681 B.C.

Shalmaneser IV, 782–773 B.C.   Esarhaddon, 681–699 B.C.

Assur-dan III, 772–755 B.C.   Ashurbanipal, 668–627 B.C.

Assur-nirari V, 754–745 B.C.

Kings of Babylon

Nabopolassar, 626–605 B.C.   Labasi-Marduk, 556 B.C.

Nebuchadnezzar II, 605–562 B.C.   Nabonidus, 555–539 B.C.

Evil-Merodach, 562–560 B.C.   (Belshazzar reigned as vice-regent)

Neriglissar, 560–556 B.C.

The Fall of Judah
(2 Kings 25)

From 605 B.C. to 586 B.C. Judah suffered repeated Babylonian invasions under the mighty leadership of Nebuchadnezzar. The final blow came from the southern approach to Jerusalem. By 560 B.C. the Empire of the Babylonians stretched from Egypt to the west to Nineveh and Susa on the east (see p. 89).

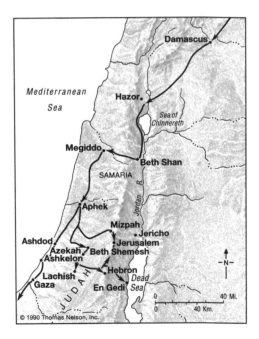

The Babylonian Empire
(560 B.C.)

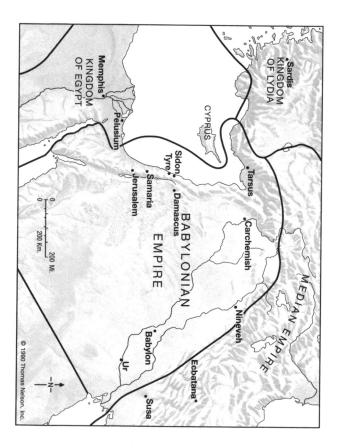

© 1990 Thomas Nelson, Inc.

Overview of First Chronicles

FOCUS	Royal Line of David			Reign of David		
REFERENCE	1:1 ———————	10:1 ———————	13:1 ———————	18:1 ———————	21:1 ———————	28:1 ——— 29:30
DIVISION	Genealogies of David and Israel	Accession of David as King	Acquisition of the Ark	Victories of David	Preparation for the Temple	Last Days of David
TOPIC	Genealogy			History		
	Ancestry			Activity		
LOCATION			Israel			
TIME	Thousands of Years			c. 33 Years		

The First Book of
CHRONICLES

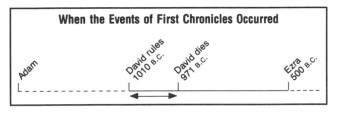

When the Events of First Chronicles Occurred

Adam — David rules 1010 B.C. — David dies 971 B.C. — Ezra 500 B.C.

LANDMARKS OF FIRST CHRONICLES

Key Word: *Priestly View of David's Reign*

Key Verses: *First Chronicles 17:11–14; 29:11*

Key Chapter: *First Chronicles 17*

Pivotal for the Book of First Chronicles as well as for the rest of the Scriptures is the Davidic Covenant recorded in Second Samuel 7 and First Chronicles 17. God promises David that He will "establish him [David's ultimate offspring, Jesus Christ] in My house and in My kingdom forever; and his throne shall be established forever" (1 Chr. 17:14).

The History of David

David was "a man after God's own heart," who desired greatly to build God's temple. The books of Samuel,

Kings and Chronicles tell and retell the story, with different emphases, as the following charts show.

The House of God Then and Now

David desires to build God's house	2 Sam. 7:5
David not allowed to build God's house	1 Chr. 28:3
David's descendant chosen to build God's house	1 Chr. 17:12
A house that will stand forever	1 Chr. 17:14
A house not built with hands	Heb. 9:11
The risen Christ; God's eternal house	John 2:19
The people of God as a holy temple	Eph. 2:19–22

Contrasts Between Chronicles and Samuel–Kings

Samuel–Kings	Chronicles
Prophetic Perspective	Priestly Perspective
Political History	Religious History
Wars Prominent	Temple Prominent
Record of Both Nations	Record of Judah
Continuing History of Nation	Continuity of David's Line
Man's Failure	God's Faithfulness

Jerusalem: David's City
(1 Chronicles 11)

David took the fortress called Jebus and renamed it the "City of David." This established his kingship militarily and politically. He then established his religious leadership by moving the ark of the covenant to the City of David.

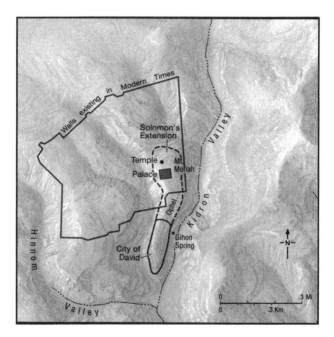

Overview of Second Chronicles

FOCUS	Reign of Solomon			Reigns of the Kings of Judah		
REFERENCE	1:1 ———————	2:1 ———————	8:1 ———————	10:1 ———————	14:1 ———————	36:1 – 36:23
DIVISION	Inauguration of Solomon	Completion of the Temple	The Glory of Solomon's Reign	The Division of the Kingdom	The Reforms Under Asa, Jehoshaphat, Joash, Hezekiah, and Josiah	The Fall of Judah
TOPIC	The Temple Is Constructed			The Temple Is Destroyed		
	Splendor			Disaster		
LOCATION	Judah					
TIME	c. 40 Years			c. 393 Years		

The Second Book of CHRONICLES

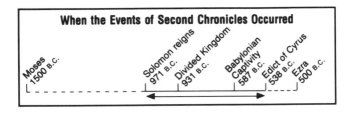

When the Events of Second Chronicles Occurred

Moses 1500 B.C. — Solomon reigns 971 B.C. — Divided Kingdom 931 B.C. — Babylonian Captivity 587 B.C. — Edict of Cyrus 538 B.C. — Ezra 500 B.C.

◆

LANDMARKS OF SECOND CHRONICLES

Key Word: *Priestly View of Judah*

The Book of Second Chronicles provides topical histories of the end of the united kingdom (Solomon) and the kingdom of Judah. More than historical annals, Chronicles is a *divine editorial* on the spiritual characteristics of the Davidic dynasty.

Key Verses: *Second Chronicles 7:14; 16:9*

Key Chapter: *Second Chronicles 34*

Second Chronicles records the reforms and revivals under such kings as Asa, Jehoshaphat, Joash, Hezekiah, and Josiah.

◆

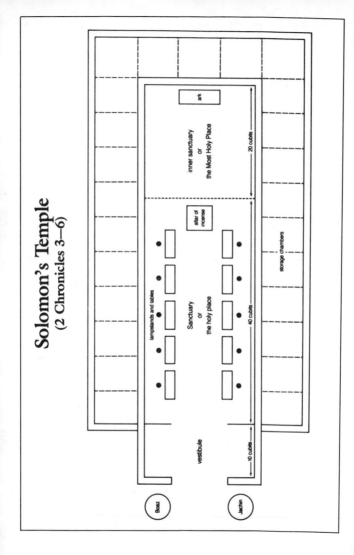

Solomon's Temple
(2 Chronicles 3–6)

ark

inner sanctuary
or
the Most Holy Place

20 cubits

altar of
incense

lampstands and tables

Sanctuary
or
the holy place

40 cubits

storage chambers

vestibule

10 cubits

Boaz

Jachin

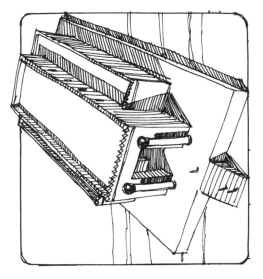

Solomon constructed the temple on Mt. Moriah, north of the ancient City of David. The temple was built according to plans that David received from the Lord and passed on to Solomon (1 Chr. 28:11–13, 19). The division into a sanctuary and inner sanctuary corresponds to the division of the tabernacle into the holy place and Most Holy Place.

Jerusalem Under Solomon

The city of Jerusalem underwent considerable expansion during the reign of Solomon. According to 1 Kings 3:1, Solomon finished building "the wall all around Jerusalem." Archaeological evidence indicates that Solomon increased the size of the city from eleven to thirty-two acres; its total population increased several times over as well. Some of the population increase was due to Solomon's family alone. He had 700 wives and 300 concubines (11:3). The number of Solomon's children is not given but must have been very large as well.

The Decline and Fall of the Divided Kingdoms

After the glories of Solomon's reign, the kingdom divided into the ten tribes of Israel and the two tribes of Judah. Second Chronicles focuses on the kings of Judah who carried out reforms until the kingdom fell in 587 B.C. The maps on pp. 100–102 contrast the area held by the divided kingdoms with that of the united kingdom at its peak under Solomon.

Jerusalem During Hezekiah's Time

The city of Jerusalem was further expanded in the time of Hezekiah, reaching a size of some 150 acres. In his efforts to fortify the city against Sennacherib, Hezekiah ordered the construction of a tunnel that would bring water from the spring of Gihon into the city proper. The tunnel was excavated through solid rock for a distance of almost 600 yards. When it was completed, it emerged just inside the southeastern corner of the old city, where what was

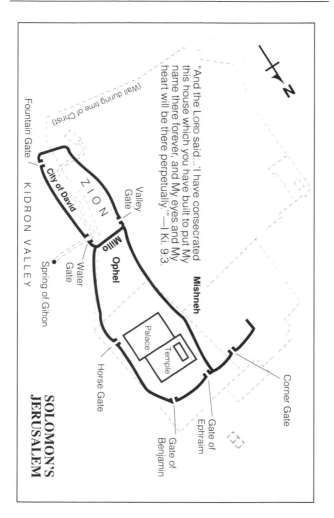

SOLOMON'S
JERUSALEM

"And the LORD said...'I have consecrated
this house which you have built to put My
name there forever, and My eyes and My
heart will be there perpetually.'" —1 Ki. 9:3.

(Wall during time of Christ)

Mishneh

ZION

City of David

Fountain Gate

KIDRON VALLEY

Valley Gate

Millo

Ophel

Water Gate

Spring of Gihon

Palace

Temple

Horse Gate

Corner Gate

Gate of Ephraim

Gate of Benjamin

The Divided Kingdom

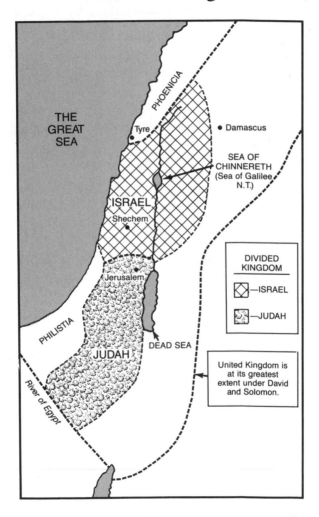

THE GREAT SEA

PHOENICIA

Tyre

• Damascus

SEA OF CHINNERETH (Sea of Galilee N.T.)

ISRAEL

Shechem

Jerusalem

PHILISTIA

DEAD SEA

JUDAH

River of Egypt

DIVIDED KINGDOM

—ISRAEL

—JUDAH

United Kingdom is at its greatest extent under David and Solomon.

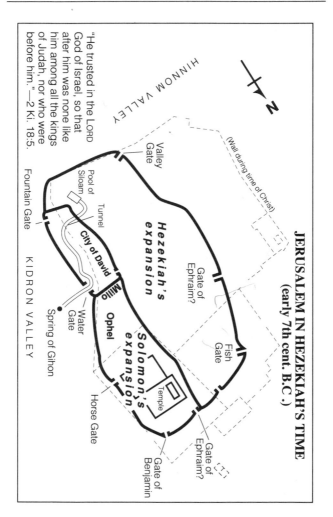

JERUSALEM IN HEZEKIAH'S TIME
(early 7th cent. B.C.)

"He trusted in the LORD God of Israel, so that after him was none like him among all the kings of Judah, nor who were before him."—2 Ki. 18:5.

HINNOM VALLEY

KIDRON VALLEY

Valley Gate

Pool of Siloam

Tunnel

City of David

Fountain Gate

Spring of Gihon

Water Gate

Millo

Hezekiah's expansion

Solomon's expansion

Ophel

(Wall during time of Christ)

Gate of Ephraim?

Fish Gate

Temple

Horse Gate

Gate of Ephraim?

Gate of Benjamin

The Spread of Solomon's Fame

Solomon's influence in economic and political affairs was enhanced by the transportation and trade routes that intersected his kingdom.

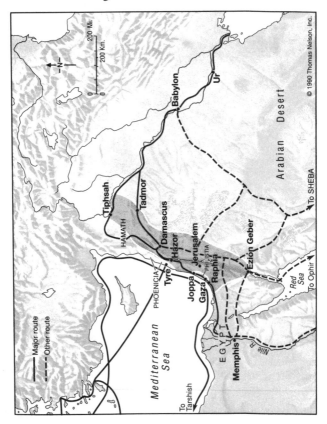

later known as the Pool of Siloam was situated. This conduit, referred to in 2 Kings 20:20 and 2 Chronicles 32:30, was a remarkable engineering accomplishment, for the excavators worked with hand tools from opposite ends, meeting in the center.

The Book of
EZRA

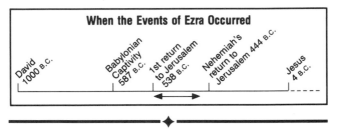

When the Events of Ezra Occurred

David 1000 B.C. — Babylonian Captivity 587 B.C. — 1st return to Jerusalem 538 B.C. — Nehemiah's return to Jerusalem 444 B.C. — Jesus 4 B.C.

LANDMARKS OF EZRA

Key Word: *Temple*

The basic theme of Ezra is the restoration of the Temple and the spiritual, moral, and social restoration of the returned remnant in Jerusalem under the leadership of Zerubbabel and Ezra.

Key Verses: *Ezra 1:3; 7:10*

Key Chapter: *Ezra 6*

Ezra 6 records the completion and dedication of the Temple which stimulates the obedience of the remnant to keep the Passover and separate themselves.

Overview of Ezra

FOCUS	Restoration of the Temple		Reformation of the People	
REFERENCE	1:1 ——————— 3:1 ———————		7:1 ——————— 9:1 ———————	10:44
DIVISION	First Return to Jerusalem	Construction of the Temple	Second Return to Jerusalem	Restoration of the People
TOPIC	Zerubbabel		Ezra	
	First Return of 49,897		Second Return of 1,754	
LOCATION	Persia to Jerusalem		Persia to Jerusalem	
TIME	22 Years (538–516 B.C.)		1 Year (458–457 B.C.)	

Route of the Jews' Return from Exile

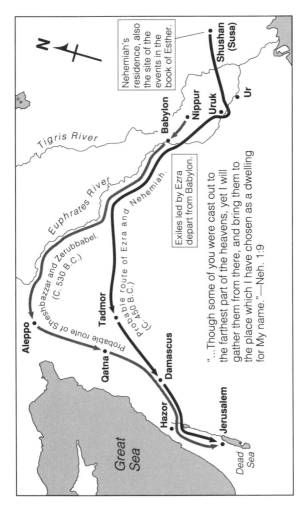

N

Nehemiah's residence, also the site of the events in the book of Esther.

Shushan (Susa)

Ur

Uruk

Nippur

Babylon

Tigris River

Euphrates River

Exiles led by Ezra and Nehemian depart from Babylon.

Probable route of Ezra and Nehemian.

Probable route of Sheshbazzar and Zerubbabel. (C. 530 B.C.)

Tadmor

Aleppo

Qatna

Damascus

Hazor

Jerusalem

Dead Sea

Great Sea

"...Though some of you were cast out to the farthest part of the heavens, yet I will gather them from there, and bring them to the place which I have chosen as a dwelling for My name."—Neh. 1:9

The Persian Empire
(500 B.C.)

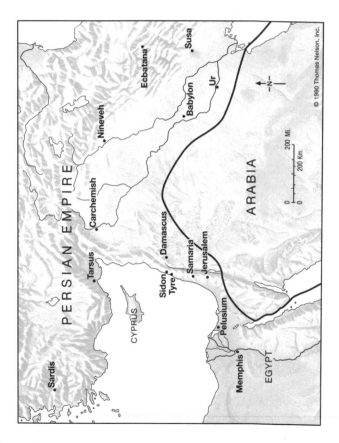

Persian Kings of the Restoration
(559–403 B. C.)

Cyrus 559–530	Cambyses 530–522	Smerdis 522	Darius I 522–486	Xerxes I (Ahasuerus) (486–465)	Artaxerxes I 465–424	Xerxes II 424	Darius II 423–404
575	550	525	500	475	450	425	400

The Relation Between the Events of Ezra, Esther, and Nehemiah

Events of the Book of Esther (483–471 BC)

Events of the Book of Nehemiah (445–ca. 425 BC)

550	525	500	475	450	425	400

Events of the Book of Ezra (538–458 B.C.)

Zerubbabel and first return of exiles: Ezra 1—6 (538 B.C.)

Ezra and second return of exiles: Ezra 7—10 (458 B.C.)

Overview of Nehemiah

FOCUS	Reconstruction of the Wall		Restoration of the People	
REFERENCE	1:1 ——— 3:1 ———	8:1 ———	11:1 ——— 13:31	
DIVISION	Preparation to Reconstruct the Wall	Reconstruction of the Wall	Renewal of the Covenant	Obedience to the Covenant
TOPIC	Political		Spiritual	
	Construction		Instruction	
LOCATION	Jerusalem			
TIME	19 Years (444–425 B.C.)			

The Book of
NEHEMIAH

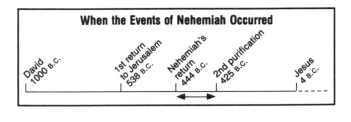

When the Events of Nehemiah Occurred

David 1000 B.C. — 1st return to Jerusalem 538 B.C. — Nehemiah's return 444 B.C. — 2nd purification 425 B.C. — Jesus 4 B.C.

LANDMARKS OF NEHEMIAH

Key Word: *Walls*

While Ezra deals with the religious restoration of Judah, Nehemiah is primarily concerned with Judah's political and geographical restoration. The first seven chapters are devoted to the rebuilding of Jerusalem's walls, because Jerusalem was the spiritual and political center of Judah. Without walls, Jerusalem could hardly be considered a city at all.

Key Verses: *Nehemiah 6:15, 16; 8:8*

Key Chapter: *Nehemiah 9*

The key to the Old Testament is the covenant, which is its theme and unifying factor. Israel's history can be divided according to the nation's obedience or disobedience to God's conditional covenant: blessings from obedience and destruction from disobedience. Nehemiah 9 records

Jerusalem in Nehemiah's Time

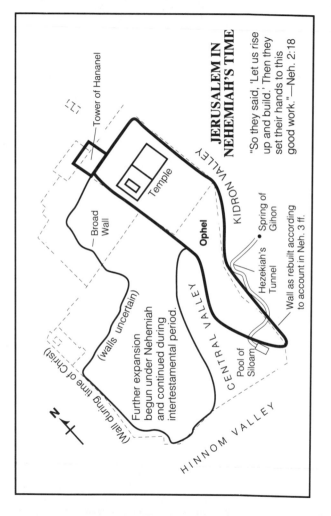

JERUSALEM IN NEHEMIAH'S TIME

"So they said, 'Let us rise up and build.' Then they set their hands to this good work." —Neh. 2:18

Tower of Hananel

Temple

Broad Wall

Ophel

KIDRON VALLEY

Spring of Gihon

Hezekiah's Tunnel

Wall as rebuilt according to account in Neh. 3 ff.

Pool of Siloam

CENTRAL VALLEY

Further expansion begun under Nehemiah and continued during intertestamental period.

(walls uncertain)

(Wall during time of Christ)

HINNOM VALLEY

N

that upon completion of the Jerusalem wall the nation reaffirmed its loyalty to the covenant.

◆

Nehemiah: A Servant	Because God . . .
Prays for his people (1:4)	*Preserves* His covenant (1:5)
Plans for his people (2:6–8)	*Places* ideas in his mind (2:12)
Perseveres against enemies for his people (4:9, 23)	*Perverts* their plans (4:15, 20)
Pleads for unity among his people (5:10, 11)	Is *pleased* with unity (5:9, 13)
Perceives falsehood and remains faithful (6:2, 8, 12)	*Proclaims* His name among the nations (6:16)

The Book of ESTHER

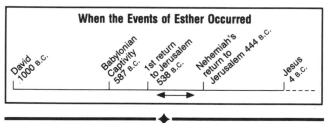

When the Events of Esther Occurred

David 1000 B.C. — Babylonian Captivity 587 B.C. — 1st return to Jerusalem 538 B.C. — Nehemiah's return to Jerusalem 444 B.C. — Jesus 4 B.C.

◆

LANDMARKS OF ESTHER

Key Word: *Providence*

The Book of Esther was written to show how the Jewish people were protected and preserved by the gracious

Overview of Esther

FOCUS	Threat to the Jews		Triumph of the Jews		
REFERENCE	1:1 ——— 2:21 ———	5:1 ———	8:4 ———	10:3	
DIVISION	Selection of Esther as Queen	Formulation of the Plot by Haman	Triumph of Mordecai over Haman	Triumph of Israel over Her Enemies	
TOPIC	Feasts of Ahasuerus		Feasts of Esther and Purim		
	Grave Danger		Great Deliverance		
LOCATION	Persia				
TIME	10 Years (483–473 B.C.)				

hand of God from the threat of annihilation. Although God disciplines His covenant people, He never abandons them.

Key Verses: *Esther 4:14; 8:17*

Key Chapter: *Esther 8*

According to the Book of Esther, the salvation of the Jews is accomplished through the second decree of King Ahasuerus, allowing the Jews to defend themselves against their enemies. Chapter 8 records this pivotal event with the accompanying result that "many of the people of the land became Jews" (8:17).

◆

Old Testament Women

One of the outstanding women of the Old Testament was Esther, a Jewish captive in Persia who saved her people from destruction by the schemer Haman (Esth. 1—10).

Other outstanding women of the Old Testament (for a New Testament list, see p. 227) include the following:

Name	Description	Biblical Reference
Bath-sheba	Wife of David; mother of Solomon	2 Sam. 11:3, 27
Deborah	Judge who defeated the Canaanites	Judg. 4:4
Delilah	Philistine who tricked Samson	Judg. 16:4, 5

continued on page 114

Name	Description	Biblical Reference
Dinah	Only daughter of Jacob	Gen. 30:21
Eve	First woman	Gen. 3:20
Gomer	Prophet Hosea's unfaithful wife	Hos. 1:2, 3
Hagar	Sarah's maid; mother of Ishmael	Gen. 16:3–16
Hannah	Mother of Samuel	1 Sam. 1
Jezebel	Wicked wife of King Ahab	1 Kin. 16:30, 31
Jochebed	Mother of Moses	Ex. 6:20
Miriam	Sister of Moses; a prophetess	Ex. 15:20
Naomi	Ruth's mother-in-law	Ruth 1:2, 4
Orpah	Ruth's sister-in-law	Ruth 1:4
Rachel	Wife of Jacob	Gen. 29:28
Rahab	Harlot who harbored Israel's spies; ancestor of Jesus	Josh. 2:3–1 Matt. 1:5
Ruth	Wife of Boaz and mother of Obed; ancestor of Jesus	Ruth 4:13, 17; Matt. 1:5
Sarah	Wife of Abraham; mother of Issac	Gen.11:29; 21:2, 3
Tamar	A daughter of David	2 Sam. 13:1
Zipporah	Wife of Moses	Ex. 2:21

Settings of the Scriptures: Important Capital Cities

Historically, the Book of Esther unveils a segment of history occurring during the Jewish captivity in Persia.

The capital Susa, or Shushan, was the centerpoint of the Persian Empire. Other capital cities mentioned in the Scriptures include:

Acmetha: Also known as Exbatana, Acmetha was capital of the Median Empire (Ezra 6:2); served as the summer residence of Persian kings.

Babylon: Capital city of the Babylonian Empire in the land of the Chaldeans (Jer. 24:5); city to which citizens of Judah were carried after the fall of Jeruaslem (2 Chr. 36:18, 20).

Damascus: Capital of Syria and important trade center; oldest continually inhabited city in the world (Gen. 14:15).

Hebron: David's capital as he ruled Judah (2 Sam. 2:1–4). Abraham's home after his return from Egypt (Gen. 13:18).

Jerusalem: Made capital of the United Kingdom by David (2 Sam. 5:6, 7); location of Solomon's temple, known as the Holy City and Zion by the Jewish people.

Nineveh: Capital of Assyria; ancient walled city was scene of the prophet Jonah's reluctant preaching mission (Jonah 3:1–3).

No: Also known as Thebes, No was capital of Egypt and center of pagan worship on banks of the Nile River (Ezek. 30:13–16).

Samaria: Permanent capital of the northern kingdom; built by Omri, a sixth king of Israel, in 800 B.C. (1 Kin. 16:23, 24).

Shechem: First capital of the northern kingdom following Solomon's reign; located in the hill country of Ephraim (Gen. 12:6).

Ur:　　　　　Capital of ancient Sumer on the Euphrates River;
　　　　　　　Abraham lived here before moving to Haran (Gen.
　　　　　　　11:31).

Miraculous Deliverances

Esther is but one remarkable story in the history of
God's redemption of His people. Other examples from
the Old Testament include:

Name	God's Action	Biblical Reference
Noah and his family	Delivered from the flood by the ark	Gen. 6–8
Lot and his family	Saved from the fiery destruction of Sodom and Gomorrah	Gen. 19:29
Nation of Israel	Delivered from Egyptian slavery through the Exodus; preserved by miraculous feedings in the Wilderness	Ex. 12–17
Israelites	Saved from fiery serpents by looking at a bronze serpent on a pole	Num. 21:6–9
David and his army	Saved from capture by Saul's army on numerous occasions	1 Sam. 23
Elijah	Fed by the ravens in the wilderness	1 Kin. 17:2–6
Three young Hebrew men	Delivered from Nebuchadnezzar's fiery furnace	Dan. 3:19–30
Daniel	Preserved, unharmed, among the lions	Dan. 6:1–24

THREE

BOOKS OF POETRY AND WISDOM

◆

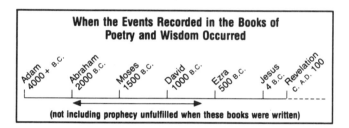

When the Events Recorded in the Books of
Poetry and Wisdom Occurred

Adam 4000 + B.C.   Abraham 2000 B.C.   Moses 1500 B.C.   David 1000 B.C.   Ezra 500 B.C.   Jesus 4 B.C.   Revelation C. A.D. 100

(not including prophecy unfulfilled when these books were written)

The Book of JOB

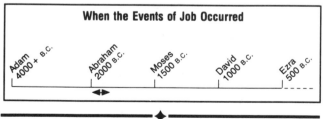

When the Events of Job Occurred

Adam 4000 + B.C.   Abraham 2000 B.C.   Moses 1500 B.C.   David 1000 B.C.   Ezra 500 B.C.

─────────────── ◆ ───────────────

LANDMARKS OF JOB

Key Word: *Sovereignty*

The basic question of the book is, "Why do the righteous suffer if God is loving and all-powerful?" Suffering

Overview of Job

FOCUS	Dilemma of Job		Debates of Job					Deliverance of Job
REFERENCE	1:1	3:1	15:1	22:1	27:1	32:1	38:1	42:17
DIVISION	Controversy of God and Satan	First Cycle of Debate	Second Cycle of Debate	Third Cycle of Debate	Final Defense of Job	Solution of Elihu	Controversy of God with Job	Repentance
TOPIC	Conflict		Debate				Prose	
	Prose		Poetry					
LOCATION	Land of Uz (North Arabia)							
TIME	Patriarchal Period (c. 2000 B.C.)							

itself is not the central theme; rather, the focus is on what Job *learns* from his suffering—the sovereignty of God over all creation.

Key Verses: *Job 13:15; 37:23, 24*

Key Chapter: *Job 42*

Upon Job's full recognition of the utter majesty and sovereignty of the Lord, he repents and no longer demands an answer as to the "why" of his plight.

---◆---

A Comparison of Theologies
(Job)

Satan	Friends
IF Job is blessed by God, THEN he will be faithful.	IF Job is faithful, THEN he will be blessed.
OR	OR
IF Job is not blessed by God, THEN he will be unfaithful. (Satan accused God of bribing His followers.)	IF Job is unfaithful, THEN he will be punished.

The Book of
PSALMS

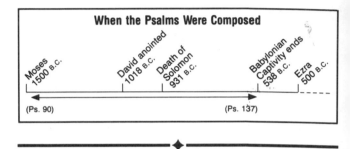

When the Psalms Were Composed

Moses 1500 B.C. — David anointed 1018 B.C. — Death of Solomon 931 B.C. — Babylonian Captivity ends 538 B.C. — Ezra 500 B.C.

(Ps. 90)   (Ps. 137)

LANDMARKS OF PSALMS

Key Word: *Worship*

The central theme of the Book of Psalms is worship—God is worthy of all praise because of who He is, what He has done, and what He will do. His goodness extends through all time and eternity.

Key Verses: *Psalm 19:14; 145:21*

Key Chapter: *Psalm 100*

So many of the favorite chapters of the Bible are contained in the Book of Psalms that it is difficult to select the key chapter among such psalms as Psalms 1; 22; 23; 24; 37; 72; 100; 101; 119; 121; and 150. The two central themes of worship and praise are beautifully wed in Psalm 100.

Overview of Psalms

BOOK	Book I (1–41)	Book II (42–72)	Book III (73–89)	Book IV (90–106)	Book V (107–150)
CHIEF AUTHOR	David	David and Korah	Asaph	Anonymous	David and Anonymous
NUMBER OF PSALMS	41	31	17	17	44
TOPICAL LIKENESS TO PENTATEUCH	Genesis: Humanity and Creation	Exodus: Deliverance and Redemption	Leviticus: Worship and Sanctuary	Numbers: Wilderness and Wandering	Deuteronomy: Scripture and Praise
BASIC CONTENT	Songs of Worship	Hymns of National Interest		Anthems of Praise	
CLOSING DOXOLOGY	41:13	72:18, 19	89:52	106:48	150:1–6
POSSIBLE COMPILER	David	Hezekiah or Josiah		Ezra or Nehemiah	
POSSIBLE DATES OF COMPILATION	c. 1020–970 B.C.	c. 970–610 B.C.		Until c. 430 B.C.	

Types of Psalms

The Book of Psalms is a collection of prayers, poems, and hymns that focus the worshiper's thoughts on God in praise and adoration. Parts of the book were used as a hymnal in the worship services of ancient Israel. The book contains 150 individual psalms, which may be grouped into the following types or categories:

Type	Psalms	Act of Worship
Individual and communal lament	3–7; 12; 13; 22; 25–28; 35; 38–40; 42–44; 51; 54–57; 59–61; 63; 64; 69–71; 74; 79; 80; 83; 85; 86; 88; 90; 102; 109; 120; 123; 130; & 140–143.	Express need for God's deliverance.
Thanksgiving	8; 18; 19; 29; 30; 32–34; 36; 40; 41; 66; 103–106; 111; 113; 116; 117; 124; 129; 135; 136; 138; 139; 146–148; & 150.	Make aware of God's blessings. Express thanks.
Enthronement	47; 93; 96–99.	Describe God's sovereign rule.
Pilgrimage	43; 46; 48; 76; 84; 87; 120–134.	Establish a mood of worship.
Royal	2; 18; 20; 21; 45; 72; 89; 101; 110; 132; & 144.	Christ the sovereign ruler portray.
Wisdom	1; 37; 119.	Instruct as to God's will.
Imprecatory	7; 35; 40; 55; 58; 59; 69; 79; 109; 137; 139; & 144.	Invoke God's wrath and judgment against his enemies.

Messianic Psalms

Many of the psalms specifically anticipate the life and ministry of Jesus Christ, the Son of David, who came centuries later as the promised Messiah. The messianic prophecies in the psalms take a variety of forms and refer to Christ in a variety of ways.

Psalm	Portrayal	Fulfilled
2:7	The Son of God	Matthew 3:17
8:2	Praised by children	Matthew 21:15, 16
8:6	Ruler of all	Hebrews 2:8
16:10	Rises from death	Matthew 28:7
22:1	Forsaken by God	Matthew 27:46
22:7, 8	Derided by enemies	Luke 23:35
22:16	Hands and feet pierced	John 20:27
22:18	Lots cast for clothes	Matthew 27:35, 36
34:20	Bones unbroken	John 19:32, 33, 36
35:11	Accused by false witnesses	Mark 14:57
35:19	Hated without cause	John 15:25
40:7, 8	Delights in God's will	Hebrews 10:7
41:9	Betrayed by a friend	Luke 22:47
45:6	The eternal King	Hebrews 1:8
68:18	Ascends to heaven	Acts 1:9–11
69:9	Zealous for God's house	John 2:17
69:21	Given vinegar and gall	Matthew 27:34
109:4	Prays for enemies	Luke 23:34
109:8	His betrayer replaced	Acts 1:20
110:1	Rules over His enemies	Matthew 22:44
110:4	A priest forever	Hebrews 5:6
118:22	The chief stone of God's building	Matthew 21:42
118:26	Comes in the name of the Lord	Matthew 21:9

Places Named in the Psalms

The Psalms were composed by a variety of authors and in various historical circumstances. They name a number of locations, many of which appear in this map.

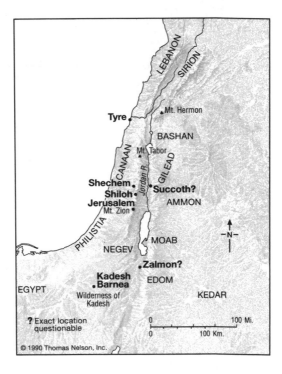

© 1990 Thomas Nelson, Inc.

The Book of
PROVERBS

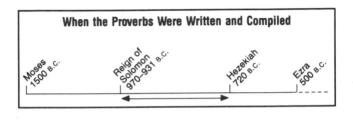

When the Proverbs Were Written and Compiled

Moses 1500 B.C.

Reign of Solomon 970–931 B.C.

Hezekiah 720 B.C.

Ezra 500 B.C.

LANDMARKS OF PROVERBS

Key Word: *Wisdom*

Proverbs is one of the few biblical books that clearly spells out its purpose. The words "wisdom and instruction" in 1:2 complement each other because *wisdom (hokhmah)* means "skill" and *instruction (musar)* means "discipline." No skill is perfected without discipline, and when a person has skill he has freedom to create something beautiful. Proverbs deals with the most fundamental skill of all: practical righteousness before God in every area of life.

Key Verses: *Proverbs 1:5–7 and 3:5, 6*

Key Chapter: *Proverbs 31*

The last chapter of Proverbs is unique in ancient literature, as it reveals a very high and noble view of women.

Overview of Proverbs

FOCUS	Purpose of Proverbs	Proverbs to Youth	Proverbs of Solomon	Proverbs of Solomon (Hezekiah)	Words of Agur	Words of Lemuel
REFERENCE	1:1 ———	1:8 ———	10:1 ———	25:1 ———	30:1 ———	31:1 ——— 31:31
DIVISION	Purpose and Theme	Father's Exhortations	First Collection of Solomon	Second Collection of Solomon	Numerical Proverbs	Virtuous Wife
TOPIC	Prologue	Principles of Wisdom			Epilogue	
	Commendation of Wisdom	Counsel of Wisdom			Comparisons of Wisdom	
LOCATION	Judah					
TIME	c. 970–720 B.C.					

Wisdom and God's Word
(Proverbs 8)

Wisdom is personified in the Proverbs and acts as God's dynamic Word. This treatment of Wisdom is an important background to the New Testament revelation of Jesus as God's Wisdom and Word. Proverbs 8 presents key qualities of God's Wisdom, summarized here in this chart.

Origin of Wisdom

In God (v. 22)
From everlasting (v. 23)
Before all things (vv. 23–30)

Teaching of Wisdom	Value of Wisdom
Prudence (vv. 5, 12)	Yields riches and honor (v. 18)
Understanding (v. 5)	Greater than gold and silver (v. 19)
Excellent things (v. 6)	
Truth (v. 7)	The wise are blessed (vv. 32, 34)
Hatred of wickedness (v. 7)	The wise find life (v. 35)
Righteousness (v. 8)	The foolish love death (v. 36)
Knowledge (v. 12)	
Discretion (v. 12)	
Fear of the Lord (v. 13)	

The Family Setting of Proverbs

Typical of Proverbs in the ancient Near East, these sayings seem to have arisen in the context of the home—evidently of the king or of his officials. Although ''son'' can also be used in the sense of "pupil," "father" and "mother" appear numerous times as well. Perhaps the most well-known chapter of Proverbs is 31, describing the virtuous wife.

The Book of
ECCLESIASTES

◆

LANDMARKS OF ECCLESIASTES

Key Word: *Vanity*

The word *vanity* appears thirty-seven times to express the many things that cannot be understood about life. All earthly goals and ambitions lead to dissatisfaction and frustration when pursued as ends in themselves apart from God.

Key Verses: *Ecclesiastes 2:24 and 12:13, 14*

Key Chapter: *Ecclesiastes 12*

Only when the Preacher views his life from God's perspective "above the sun" does it take on meaning as a precious gift "from the hand of God" (2:24). Chapter 12 resolves the book's extensive inquiry into the meaning of life with the single conclusion, "Fear God and keep His commandments, for this is the whole duty of man" (12:13).

◆

Overview of Ecclesiastes

FOCUS						
	Thesis: "All Is Vanity"		Proof: "Life Is Vain"			Counsel: "Fear God"
REFERENCE 1:1 ———	1:4 ———	1:12 ———	3:1 ———	7:1 ———	10:1 ——— 12:9 ——— 12:14	
DIVISION	Introduction of Vanity	Illustrations of Vanity	Proof from Scripture	Proof from Observations	Coping in a Wicked World	Counsel for Uncertainty	Conclusion: Fear and Obey God
	Declaration of Vanity		Demonstration of Vanity		Decision from Vanity		
TOPIC	Subject		Sermons		Summary		
LOCATION	Universe: "Under the Sun"						
TIME	c. 935 B.C.						

The Way of Wisdom
(Ecclesiastes)

Without God "all is vanity"

Godless learning .... cynicism (1:7, 8)
Godless greatness .... sorrow (1:16–18)
Godless pleasure .... disappointment (2:1, 2)
Godless labor .... hatred of life (2:17)
Godless philosophy .... emptiness (3:1–9)
Godless eternity .... unfulfillment (3:11)
Godless life .... depression (4:2, 3)
Godless religion .... dread (5:7)
Godless wealth .... trouble (5:12)
Godless existence .... frustration (6:12)
Godless wisdom .... despair (11:1–8)

With God

GODLY FEAR .... FULFILLMENT (12:13, 14)

The Song of
SOLOMON

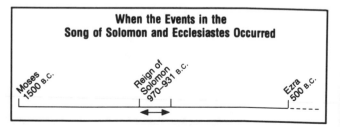

**When the Events in the
Song of Solomon and Ecclesiastes Occurred**

Moses 1500 B.C.   Reign of Solomon 970–931 B.C.   Ezra 500 B.C.

Overview of the Song of Solomon

FOCUS	Beginning of Love		Broadening of Love		
REFERENCE	1:1 ———	3:6 ———	5:2 ———	7:11 ———	8:14
DIVISION	Falling in Love	United in Love	Struggling in Love	Growing in Love	
TOPIC	Courtship	Wedding	Problem	Progress	
	Fostering of Love	Fulfillment of Love	Frustration of Love	Faithfulness of Love	
LOCATION	Israel				
TIME	c. 1 Year				

LANDMARKS OF SONG OF SOLOMON

Key Word: *Love in Marriage*

The purpose of this book depends on the viewpoint taken as to its primary thrust:

Fictional: To portray Solomon's attraction and marriage to a poor but beautiful girl from the country.

Allegorical: To present God's love for His bride Israel or Christ's love for His Church.

Historical: To record Solomon's actual romance with a Shulamite woman. The various scenes in the book exalt the joys of love in courtship and marriage and offers a proper perspective of human love.

Key Verses: *Song of Solomon 7:10 and 8:7*

FOUR

BOOKS OF THE MAJOR PROPHETS

◆

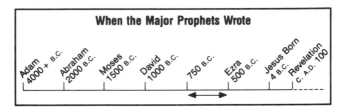

When the Major Prophets Wrote

Adam 4000+ B.C. | Abraham 2000 B.C. | Moses 1500 B.C. | David 1000 B.C. | 750 B.C. | Ezra 500 B.C. | Jesus Born 4 B.C. | Revelation c. A.D. 100

The Prophets of Israel and Judah

From the Scriptures we learn where some of the prophets were born or where they prophesied. (The chart on p. 135 shows when each writing prophet may have prophesied.)

Samuel, who served as prophet and judge, used his hometown of Ramah as a base from which he made his yearly circuit to other places. Two other prophets of the early monarchy, Elijah and Elisha, had their homes in the northern kingdom.

Among the "writing prophets," only Hosea and Jonah were from the North. The exact location of Hosea's home and ministry are unknown. Jonah was from Gath Hepher, but his ministry extended beyond his homeland to the foreign city of Nineveh.

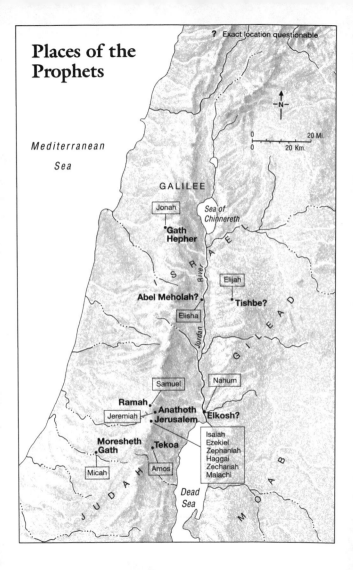

Places of the Prophets

? Exact location questionable

Mediterranean Sea

GALILEE

Jonah
Gath Hepher

Sea of Chinnereth

Elijah

Abel Meholah?

Tishbe?

Elisha

Jordan River

GILEAD

Nahum

Samuel

Ramah

Jeremiah

Anathoth
Jerusalem

Elkosh?

Moresheth Gath

Tekoa

Isaiah
Ezekiel
Zephaniah
Haggai
Zechariah
Malachi

Micah

Amos

Dead Sea

JUDAH

MOAB

ISRAEL

Some prophets had homes in the South, but prophesied to the North. Amos came from Tekoa but preached against the northern kingdom's worship at Bethel. Micah's message addressed Israel as well as Judah.

The Times of the Prophets

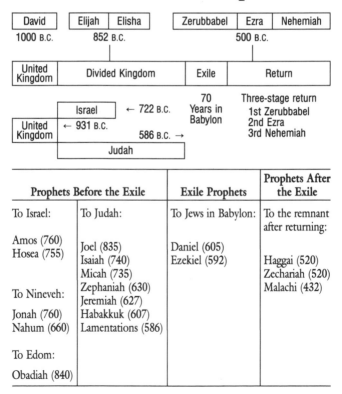

David	Elijah	Elisha		Zerubbabel	Ezra	Nehemiah
1000 B.C.	852 B.C.			500 B.C.		

United Kingdom	Divided Kingdom	Exile	Return

	Israel	← 722 B.C.	70 Years in Babylon	Three-stage return
United Kingdom	← 931 B.C.	586 B.C. →		1st Zerubbabel 2nd Ezra 3rd Nehemiah
	Judah			

Prophets Before the Exile		Exile Prophets	Prophets After the Exile
To Israel:	To Judah:	To Jews in Babylon:	To the remnant after returning:
Amos (760) Hosea (755)	Joel (835) Isaiah (740) Micah (735) Zephaniah (630) Jeremiah (627) Habakkuk (607) Lamentations (586)	Daniel (605) Ezekiel (592)	Haggai (520) Zechariah (520) Malachi (432)
To Nineveh: Jonah (760) Nahum (660)			
To Edom: Obadiah (840)			

The ministry of several prophets centers on Judah and the capital city of Jerusalem. The messages of Isaiah, Jeremiah, Zephaniah, Ezekiel, Haggai, Zechariah, and Malachi span a long time period, but all concern either Jerusalem's approaching destruction, fall, or later rebuilding.

For some prophets, such as Joel, Obadiah, and Habakkuk, geographical information is lacking. The home of Nahum is indicated only by his designation as "the Elkoshite."

The Book of
ISAIAH

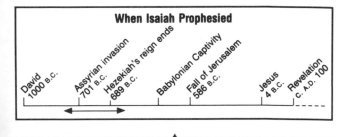

When Isaiah Prophesied

David 1000 B.C. — Assyrian invasion 701 B.C. — Hezekiah's reign ends 689 B.C. — Babylonian Captivity — Fall of Jerusalem 586 B.C. — Jesus 4 B.C. — Revelation c. A.D. 100

LANDMARKS OF ISAIAH

Key Word: *Salvation Is of the Lord*

The basic theme of this book, sometimes called "the fifth gospel," is found in Isaiah's name: "Salvation Is of the Lord." Humanity has great need for salvation, and only God's great provision will suffice.

Key Verses: *Isaiah 9:6, 7 and 53:6*

Overview of Isaiah

FOCUS	Prophecies of Condemnation				Historical Parenthesis	Prophecies of Comfort		
REFERENCE	1:1 ——	13:1 ——	24:1 ——	28:1 ——	36:1 ——	40:1 ——	49:1 ——	58:1 —— 66:24
DIVISION	Prophecies Against		Prophecies of		Hezekiah's Salvation, Sickness, and Sin	Israel's Deliverance	Israel's Deliverer	Israel's Glorious Future
	Judah	The Nations	Day of Lord	Judgment & Blessing				
TOPIC	Prophetic				Historic	Messianic		
	Judgment				Transition	Hope		
LOCATION	Israel and Judah							
TIME	c. 740–680 B.C.							

Key Chapter: *Isaiah 53*

Along with Psalm 22, Isaiah 53 lists the most remarkable and specific prophecies of the atonement of the Messiah.

◆

The Messiah King
(Isaiah 11)

Even in the midst of his prophecies of judgment, Isaiah described the ideal King whose rule would contrast with the dark reign of King Ahaz (Isa. 7; 2 Chr. 28:1–4). The role remained unfulfilled until the coming of Jesus the Messiah.

The Messiah		His Kingdom	
The Branch, a descendant of David, the stem of Jesse	11:1, 10	The Gentiles will seek Him	11:10
God's Spirit will rest upon Him	11:2	The remnant of Israel will be gathered	11:11–16
He will fear the Lord	11:3	There will be joy in God's salvation	12:1–6
He will judge the earth with righteousness	11:4, 5		

The Suffering Servant
(Isaiah 52—53)

Isaiah 52:13—53:12, the final of four Servant Songs (42:1–4; 49:1–6; 50:4–9), describes the saving work of

the Servant in five stanzas: His humiliation and rejection
(52:13–15); His rejection (53:1–3); His suffering (53:4–
6); His death (53:7–9); and His atonement (53:10–12).
This chart notes specific descriptions of the Servant and
the New Testament witness to their fulfillment in Jesus
Christ:

The Prophecy	The Fulfillment
He will be exalted (52:13)	Phil. 2:9
He will be disfigured by suffering (52:14; 53:2)	Mark 15:17, 19
He will make a blood atonement (52:15)	1 Pet. 1:2
He will be widely rejected (53:1, 3)	John 12:37, 28
He will bear our sins and sorrows (53:4, 5)	Rom. 4:25; 1 Pet. 2:24, 25
He will be our substitute (53:6, 8)	2 Cor. 5:21
He will voluntarily accept our guilt and punishment (53:7, 8)	John 10:11; 19:30
He will be buried in a rich man's tomb (53:9)	John 19:38–42
He will save us who believe in Him (53:10, 11)	John 3:16; Acts 16:31
He will die on behalf of transgressors (53:12)	Mark 15:27, 28; Luke 22:37

The Book of JEREMIAH

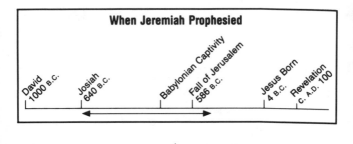

When Jeremiah Prophesied

David 1000 B.C.

Josiah 640 B.C.

Babylonian Captivity

Fall of Jerusalem 586 B.C.

Jesus Born 4 B.C.

Revelation C. A.D. 100

◆

LANDMARKS OF JEREMIAH

Key Word: *Judah's Last Hour*

In Jeremiah, God is seen as patient and holy: He delays judgment and appeals to His people to repent before it is too late. Judah's time for repentance will soon pass.

Key Verses: *Jeremiah 7:23, 24 and 8:11, 12*

Key Chapter: *Jeremiah 31*

Amid all the judgment and condemnation by Jeremiah are the wonderful promises of Jeremiah 31. Even though Judah has broken the covenants of her great King, God will make a new covenant and write it on their hearts.

◆

Overview of Jeremiah

FOCUS	Call of Jeremiah	Prophecies to Judah						Prophecies to the Gentiles	Fall of Jerusalem
REFERENCE	1:1 ———	2:1 ———	26:1 ———	30:1 ———		34:1 ———		46:1 ———	52:1 —— 52:34
DIVISION	Prophetic Commission	Condemnation of Judah	Conflicts of Jeremiah	Future Restoration of Jerusalem		Present Fall of Jerusalem		Condemnation of Nine Nations	Historic Conclusion
TOPIC	Call	Before the Fall				The Fall		After the Fall	Retrospect
		Ministry							
LOCATION		Judah						Surrounding Nations	Babylon
TIME	c. 640–580 B.C.								

Jeremiah's Journey to Egypt

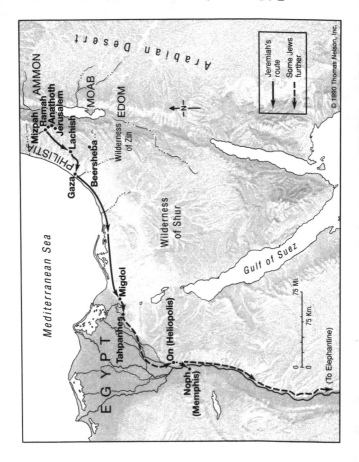

The Call of Jeremiah
(1:9, 10)

Who?	The son of Hilkiah (1:1)
Where?	Anathoth in Benjamin (1:1)
When?	The reign of Josiah, 626 B.C. (1:2)
Why?	Ordained a prophet to the nations (1:5)
Origin?	Decided before his birth (1:5)
Jeremiah's response	"I am a youth" (1:6)
God corrects him	"I am with you" (1:7, 8)
God enables him	Given words of power (1:9, 10)

The dramatic character of Jeremiah's call highlights the principle that when God calls a person to a task, He also equips that person for the task. Like Jeremiah, we list our weaknesses and limitations, but God promises His enabling presence. Like Jeremiah, we anticipate fearful situations, but God promises His deliverance. God does not call us to a task he cannot help us to fulfill.

The Scope of Jeremiah

The "weeping prophet," Jeremiah, served during the final years of the southern Kingdom of Judah. While most of the Book of Jeremiah concerns Judah, chapters 46—51 contain prophecies against nine nations—from Egypt in the south, to Damascus in the north and Babylon to the east. After the fall of Jerusalem, Jeremiah was sent by God to Egypt, where presumably he died.

The Book of
LAMENTATIONS

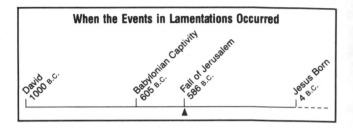

When the Events in Lamentations Occurred

David 1000 B.C. — Babylonian Captivity 605 B.C. — Fall of Jerusalem 586 B.C. — Jesus Born 4 B.C.

LANDMARKS OF LAMENTATIONS

Key Word: *Lamentations*

Three themes run through the five laments of Jeremiah. The most prominent is the theme of mourning but with confession of sin and an acknowledgment of God's righteous judgment comes a note of hope in God's future restoration of His people.

Key Verses: *Lamentations 2:5, 6 and 3:22, 23*

Key Chapter: *Lamentations 3*

Lamentations 3:22–25 expresses a magnificent faith in the mercy of God—especially when placed against the dark backdrop of chapters 1, 2, 4, and 5.

Overview of Lamentations

FOCUS	Destruction of Jerusalem	Anger of Jehovah	Prayer for Mercy	Siege of Jerusalem	Prayer for Restoration
REFERENCE	1:1 ——————	2:1 ——————	3:1 ——————	4:1 ——————	5:1 —————— 5:22
DIVISION	Mourning City	Broken People	Suffering Prophet	Ruined Kingdom	Penitent Nation
TOPIC	Grief	Cause	Hope	Repentance	Prayer
LOCATION	Jerusalem				
TIME	c. 586 B.C.				

The Road to Renewal
(Lamentations)

The author of Lamentations grieves over the suffering the people brought on themselves through rebellion against God, but take hope in the confidence that God will lead his people back to Himself.

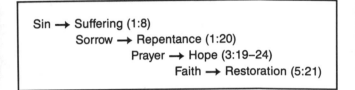

Sin → Suffering (1:8)
    Sorrow → Repentance (1:20)
        Prayer → Hope (3:19–24)
            Faith → Restoration (5:21)

The Book of EZEKIEL

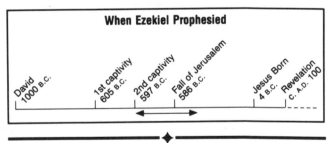

When Ezekiel Prophesied

David 1000 B.C.   1st captivity 605 B.C.   2nd captivity 597 B.C.   Fall of Jerusalem 586 B.C.   Jesus Born 4 B.C.   Revelation c. A.D. 100

LANDMARKS OF EZEKIEL

Key Word: *The Future Restoration of Israel*

The broad purpose of Ezekiel is to remind the generation born during the Babylonian exile of the cause of

Overview of Ezekiel

FOCUS	Commission of Ezekiel		Judgment on Judah	Judgment on Gentiles	Restoration of Israel	
REFERENCE	1:1 ———	2:1 ———	4:1 ———	25:1 ———	33:1 ———	40:1 ——— 48:35
DIVISION	Ezekiel Sees the Glory	Ezekiel Is Commissioned to the Work	Signs, Messages, Visions, and Parables of Judgment	Judgment on Surrounding Nations	Return of Israel to the Lord	Restoration of Israel in the Kingdom
TOPIC	Before the Siege (c. 592–587 B.C.)			During the Siege (c. 586 B.C.)	After the Siege (c. 585–570 B.C.)	
	Judah's Fall			Judah's Foes	Judah's Future	
LOCATION	Babylon					
TIME	c. 597–573 B.C.					

The Temple Complex

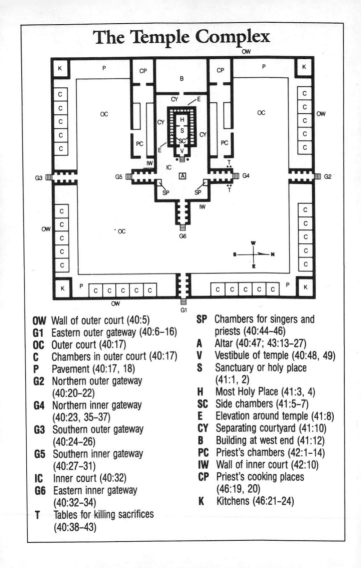

OW	Wall of outer court (40:5)	**SP** Chambers for singers and priests (40:44–46)
G1	Eastern outer gateway (40:6–16)	**A** Altar (40:47; 43:13–27)
OC	Outer court (40:17)	**V** Vestibule of temple (40:48, 49)
C	Chambers in outer court (40:17)	**S** Sanctuary or holy place (41:1, 2)
P	Pavement (40:17, 18)	**H** Most Holy Place (41:3, 4)
G2	Northern outer gateway (40:20–22)	**SC** Side chambers (41:5–7)
G4	Northern inner gateway (40:23, 35–37)	**E** Elevation around temple (41:8)
G3	Southern outer gateway (40:24–26)	**CY** Separating courtyard (41:10)
G5	Southern inner gateway (40:27–31)	**B** Building at west end (41:12)
IC	Inner court (40:32)	**PC** Priest's chambers (42:1–14)
G6	Eastern inner gateway (40:32–34)	**IW** Wall of inner court (42:10)
T	Tables for killing sacrifices (40:38–43)	**CP** Priest's cooking places (46:19, 20)
		K Kitchens (46:21–24)

Israel's current destruction, of the coming judgment on the Gentile nations, and of the coming national restoration of Israel.

Key Verses: *Ezekiel 36:24–26 and 36:33–35*

Key Chapter: *Ezekiel 37*

Central to the hope of the restoration of Israel is the vision of the valley of the dry bones. Ezekiel 37 outlines with clear steps Israel's future.

◆

Ezekiel's Temple

Ezekiel 40 presents a detailed plan for a new temple complex in Jerusalem. Some interpret this prophecy as an exact blueprint of a physical temple to be constructed in or near Jerusalem during a future millennial (thousand-year) period. Others view Ezekiel's restored temple not as a

continued on page 152

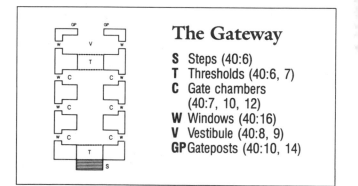

The Gateway

S Steps (40:6)
T Thresholds (40:6, 7)
C Gate chambers (40:7, 10, 12)
W Windows (40:16)
V Vestibule (40:8, 9)
GP Gateposts (40:10, 14)

The Near East of Ezekiel's Time

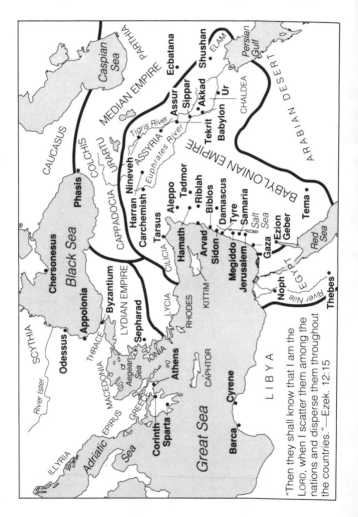

"Then they shall know that I am the LORD, when I scatter them among the nations and disperse them throughout the countries."—Ezek. 12:15

The Restoration of the Land
(Ezekiel 47)

HAMATH
Zedad
Hazar Enan
DAN
Berothah
ASHER
MANSUATE
NAPHTALI
Damascus
Mediterranean Sea
MANASSEH
KARNAIM
Sea of Chinnereth
MEGIDDO
EPHRAIM
HAURAN
REUBEN
SAMARIA
GILEAD
Jordan River
JUDAH
AMMON
Jerusalem
BENJAMIN
Dead Sea
SIMEON
ISSACHAR
MOAB
ZEBULUN
Tamar
EDOM
GAD
Meribah of Kadesh
PHILISTIA

—N—

The boundaries of the restored nation of Israel approach the boundaries of the land as it was under David and Solomon. However, the tribes are not arranged as they were historically when the land was divided under Joshua (Josh. 13–19). God will do something new in the restoration.

blueprint, but as a vision that stresses the purity and spiritual vitality of the ideal place of worship and those who will worship there. Thus, it is not intended to refer to an earthly, physical fulfillment, but express the truth found in the name of the new city: THE LORD IS THERE (48:35).

The Book of
DANIEL

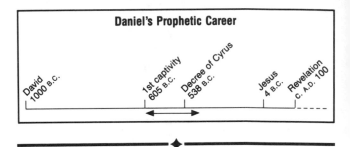

Daniel's Prophetic Career

David 1000 B.C. — 1st captivity 605 B.C. — Decree of Cyrus 538 B.C. — Jesus 4 B.C. — Revelation C. A.D. 100

LANDMARKS OF DANIEL

Key Word: *God's Program for Israel*

Daniel was written to encourage the exiled Jews by revealing God's sovereign program for Israel during and after the period of gentile domination. The "Times of the Gentiles" began with the Babylonian captivity, and Israel would suffer under gentile powers for many years. But this period is not permanent, and a time will come when God will establish the messianic kingdom which will last forever.

Overview of Daniel

FOCUS	History of Daniel	Prophetic Plan for the Gentiles				Prophetic Plan of Israel			
REFERENCE	1:1 —————— 2:1 ——————		5:1 ——	6:1 ——	7:1 ——	8:1 ——	9:1 ——	10:1 ——12:13	
DIVISION	Personal Life of Daniel	Visions of Nebuchadnezzar	Vision of Belshazzar	Decree of Darius	Four Beasts	Vision of Ram and Male-Goat	Vision of Seventy Weeks	Vision of Israel's Future	
DIVISION	Daniel's Background	Daniel Interprets Others' Dreams				Angel Interprets Daniel's Dreams			
TOPIC	Hebrew	Aramaic				Hebrew			
LOCATION	Babylon or Persia								
TIME	c. 605–536 B.C.								

Dreams and Visions in Daniel

Image—Chapter 2	Beasts—Chapter 7	Beasts—Chapter 8	Kingdoms Represented
Head of fine gold	Like a lion with eagle's wings		Babylon
Chest and arms of silver	Like a bear	Ram with two horns	Medo-Persia
Belly and thighs of bronze	Like a leopard with four wings and four heads	Male goat with one great horn, four horns and little horn	Greece
Legs of iron, feet of iron and clay	Incomparable beast with ten horns and little horn		Rome
Stone that becomes a great mountain	Messiah and saints receive the kingdom		Kingdom of God

The Times of the Gentiles

Alexander's Greek Empire
(Daniel 2, 7, 8, 11)

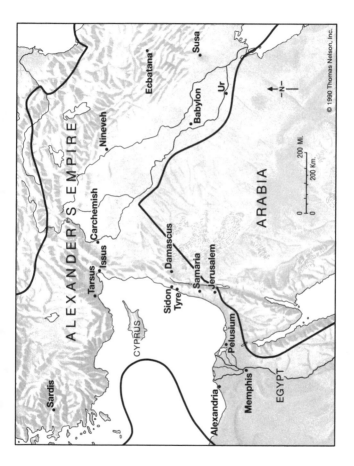

Key Verses: *Daniel 2:20–22 and Daniel 2:44*

Key Chapter: *Daniel 9*

Daniel's prophecy of the seventy weeks (9:24–27) provides the chronological frame for messianic prediction from the time of Daniel to the establishment of the kingdom on earth.

———————————◆———————————

FIVE

BOOKS OF THE MINOR PROPHETS

◆

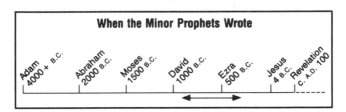

When the Minor Prophets Wrote

Adam 4000+ B.C. | Abraham 2000 B.C. | Moses 1500 B.C. | David 1000 B.C. | Ezra 500 B.C. | Jesus 4 B.C. | Revelation C. A.D. 100

The Book of HOSEA

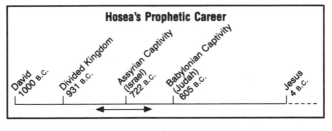

Hosea's Prophetic Career

David 1000 B.C. | Divided Kingdom 931 B.C. | Assyrian Captivity (Israel) 722 B.C. | Babylonian Captivity (Judah) 605 B.C. | Jesus 4 B.C.

◆

LANDMARKS OF HOSEA
Key Word: *The Loyal Love of God for Israel*

The themes of chapters 1—3 echo throughout the rest of the book. The adultery of Gomer (chap. 1) illustrates

Overview of Hosea

FOCUS	Adulterous Wife and Faithful Husband		Adulterous Israel and Faithful Lord			
REFERENCE	1:1 ——————— 2:2 ———————	3:1 ———————	4:1 ———————	6:4 ———————	9:1 ——————— 11:1 ——————— 14:9	
DIVISION	Prophetic Marriage	Application of Gomer to Israel	Restoration of Gomer	Spiritual Adultery of Israel	Refusal of Israel to Repent	Judgment of Israel by God	Restoration of Israel to God
TOPIC	Marriage of Hosea			Message of Hosea		
	Personal			National		
LOCATION	Northern Kingdom of Israel					
TIME	c. 755–715 B.C.					

the sin of Israel (chaps. 4—7); the degradation of Gomer (chap. 2) represents the judgment of Israel (chaps. 8—10); and Hosea's redemption of Gomer (chap. 3) pictures the restoration of Israel (chaps. 11—14). More than any other Old Testament prophet, Hosea's personal experiences illustrate his prophetic message.

Key Verses: *Hosea 4:1; 11:7-9*

Key Chapter: *Hosea 4*

The nation of Israel has left the knowledge of the truth and followed the idolatrous ways of their pagan neighbors. Central to the book is Hosea 4:6.

◆

What's in a Name?
(Hosea 1)

Names play a significant part in understanding Hosea, as the chart describes:

Name	Meaning
Jezreel (Hos. 1:4)	God Scatters
Lo-Ruhamah (Hos. 1:6)	Not Pitied
Lo-Amni (Hos. 1:9)	Not My People
Hosea (Hos. 1:1, related also to *Joshua*, Num. 13:16, and *Jesus*, Matt. 1:21)	Yahweh Is Salvation

Israel's Apostasy and
Hosea's Marriage

The stages of Israel's relationship with God are depicted in the prophecies of Jeremiah and Ezekiel, as well as in Hosea's relationship with Gomer.

Hosea's Experience	Israel's Prophets
Betrothal (1:2)	Jeremiah 2:2
Marriage (1:3)	Ezekiel 16:8–14
Adultery (3:1)	Jeremiah 5:7; Ezekiel 16:15–34
Estrangement (3:3, 4)	Jeremiah 3:8–10; Ezekiel 16:35–52
Restoration (3:5)	Ezekiel 16:53–63

The Book of
JOEL

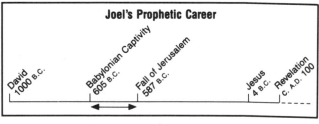

Joel's Prophetic Career

♦

LANDMARKS OF JOEL

Key Word: *The Great and Terrible Day of the Lord*

The key theme of Joel is the day of the Lord in retrospect and prospect. Joel uses the terrible locust plague that

Overview of Joel

FOCUS	Day of the Lord in Retrospect			Day of the Lord in Prospect	
REFERENCE	1:1 ———————	1:13 ———————	2:1	——————— 2:28	——————— 3:21
DIVISION	Past Day of the Locust	Past Day of the Drought	Imminent Day of the Lord	Ultimate Day of the Lord	
TOPIC	Historical Invasion		Prophetic Invasion		
	Past Judgment on Judah		Future Judgment and Restoration of Judah		
LOCATION	Southern Kingdom of Judah				
TIME	c. 600 B.C.				

has recently occurred in Judah to illustrate the coming day of judgment.

Key Verses: *Joel 2:11, 28, 29*

Key Chapter: *Joel 2*

The prophet calls for Judah's repentance and promises God's repentance (2:13, 14) from His planned judgment upon Judah if they do indeed turn to Him.

---◆---

The Book of AMOS

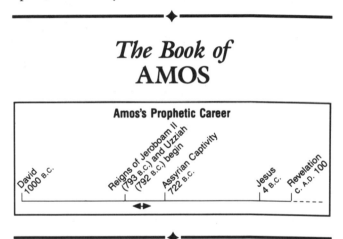

Amos's Prophetic Career

David 1000 B.C.

Reigns of Jeroboam II (793 B.C.) and Uzziah (792 B.C.) begin

Assyrian Captivity 722 B.C.

Jesus 4 B.C.

Revelation C. A.D. 100

---◆---

LANDMARKS OF AMOS

Key Word: *The Judgment of Israel*

The basic theme of Amos is the coming judgment of Israel because of the holiness of God and the sinfulness of His covenant people.

Key Verses: *Amos 3:1, 2; 8:11, 12*

Overview of Amos

FOCUS		Eight Prophecies		Three Sermons		Five Visions		Five Promises
REFERENCE	1:1 ———		3:1 ———		7:1 ———		9:11 ———	9:15
DIVISION		Judgment of Israel and Surrounding Nations	Sin of Israel: Present, Past, and Future		Pictures of the Judgment of Israel		Restoration of Israel	
TOPIC		Pronouncements of Judgment	Provocations for Judgment		Future of Judgment		Promises After Judgment	
		Judgment					Hope	
LOCATION		Surrounding Nations	Northern Kingdom of Israel					
TIME		c. 760–753 B.C.						

Key Chapter: *Amos 9*

Set in the midst of the harsh judgments of Amos are some of the greatest prophecies of restoration of Israel anywhere in Scripture. Within the scope of just five verses the future of Israel becomes clear, as the Abrahamic, Davidic, and Palestinian covenants are focused on their climactic fulfillment in the return of the Messiah.

◆

The Preservation of the Remnant
(Amos)

In the eighth century B.C., Amos prophesied Israel's doom (8:1, 2), but he also declared the possibility of deliverance for the "remnant of Joseph" (5:15). Throughout history God has always preserved a remnant of His people, as the following chart shows.

People or Group	Reference
Noah and family in the Flood	Gen. 7:1
Joseph in Egypt during the famine	Gen. 45:7
Israel to their homeland	Deut. 4:27–31
7,000 who had not worshiped Baal	1 Kin. 19:18
Portion of Judah after captivity	Isa. 10:20–23
Remnant to Zion	Mic. 2:12, 13
The church—both Jews and Gentiles	Rom. 9:22–27

Judgment Against Eight Nations

The phrase "For three trangressions . . . and for four" is a literary device to communicate "fullness (three) to overflowing (four)." The judgment spirals out from Judah and Israel to the surrounding nations.

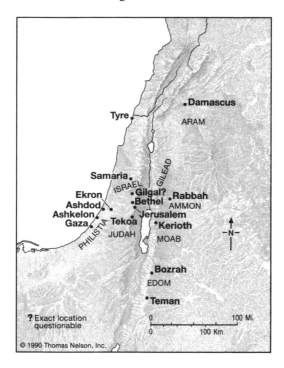

The Book of
OBADIAH

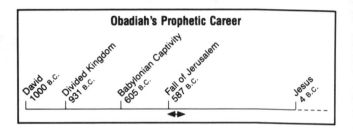

Obadiah's Prophetic Career

David 1000 B.C. | Divided Kingdom 931 B.C. | Babylonian Captivity 605 B.C. | Fall of Jerusalem 587 B.C. | Jesus 4 B.C.

LANDMARKS OF OBADIAH

Key Word: *The Judgment of Edom*

The major theme of Obadiah is a declaration of Edom's coming doom because of its arrogance and cruelty to Judah.

Key Verses: *Obadiah 10 and 21*

Overview of Obadiah

FOCUS	Judgment of Edom			Restoration of Israel
REFERENCE	1:1 ———————	10 ———————	15 ———————	19 ——————— 21
DIVISION	Predictions of Judgment	Reasons for Judgment	Results of Judgment	Possession of Edom by Israel
TOPIC		Defeat of Israel		Victory of Israel
	Prediction of Judgment			Prediction of Possession
LOCATION	Edom and Israel			
TIME	c. 586–539 B.C.			

The Book of
JONAH

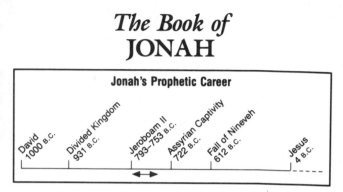

Jonah's Prophetic Career

David
1000 B.C.

Divided Kingdom
931 B.C.

Jeroboam II
793–753 B.C.

Assyrian Captivity
722 B.C.

Fall of Nineveh
612 B.C.

Jesus
4 B.C.

(See map, "The Assyrian Empire," p. 86, to identify the location of Nineveh within the powerful empire that threatened Judah at the time of Jonah.)

---◆---

LANDMARKS OF JONAH

Key Word: *The Revival in Nineveh*

God's loving concern for the Gentiles is not a truth disclosed only in the New Testament. More than seven centuries before Christ, God commissioned the Hebrew prophet Jonah to proclaim a message of repentance to the Assyrians.

Key Verses: *Jonah 2:8, 9; 4:2*

Key Chapter: *Jonah 3*

The third chapter of Jonah records perhaps the greatest revival of all time as the entire city of Nineveh "[believes] God, and [proclaims] a fast," and cries out to God.

---◆---

Overview of Jonah

FOCUS	First Commission of Jonah			Second Commission of Jonah		
REFERENCE	1:1 ——	1:4 ——	2:1 —— 2:10 ——	3:1 ——	3:5 ——	4:1 —— 4:4 —— 4:11
DIVISION	Disobedience to the First Call	Judgment on Jonah Exacted	Prayer of Jonah in the Fish / Deliverance of Jonah from the Fish	Obedience to the Second Call	Judgment on Nineveh Averted	Prayer of Jonah / Rebuke of Jonah
TOPIC	"I Won't Go."	God's Mercy upon Jonah	"I Will Go."	"I'm Here."	God's Mercy upon Nineveh	"I Shouldn't Have Come."
LOCATION	The Great Sea			The Great City		
TIME	c. 760 B.C.					

Contrasting Jonah and the Mariners
(Jonah 1)

Jonah	The Mariners
He was a Hebrew with a rich history of YAHWEH God's faithfulness.	They were Gentiles with no history of YAHWEH God.
He was monotheistic, believing in the one true God. (v. 9)	They were polytheistic, worshiping many false gods.
He was rightly related to the true God.	They had no relationship with the true God.
He was spiritually insensitive, going in the wrong direction from God. (v. 5)	They were spiritually sensitive, moving in the right direction towards God. They prayed. (v. 5)
He was indifferent toward God's will in spite of knowing Him.	They were concerned before God in spite of little or no knowledge of Him.
He was uncompassionate toward Nineveh. (v. 3)	They were compassionate toward Jonah. (vv. 11–14)
Jonah was rebellious and therefore disciplined, but not destroyed. (v. 17)	They were brought to worship and commitment. (v. 16)

God and Nineveh vs. Jonah and the Plant

God and Nineveh	Jonah and the Plant
God cared for the people of Nineveh	Jonah cared for a plant
God was concerned for the welfare of others	Jonah was concerned for himself
God created all that was in Nineveh	Jonah did not create the plant
God tended Nineveh	Jonah did nothing for the plant
The people of Nineveh are of *eternal* significance	The plant was *most temporal*.
God's concern was and is for human life	Jonah's concern was for personal comfort and selfish personal interest
God's concern for Nineveh is proper and displays his love	Jonah's concern for a plant rather than for people is improper; it displays selfishness and an improper perspective on life

Overview of Micah

FOCUS	Prediction of Judgment		Prediction of Restoration			Plea for Repentance		
REFERENCE	1:1 ——— 3:1 ———		4:1 ——— 4:6 ———		5:2 ——— 6:1 ———	6:10 ——— 7:7 ——— 7:20		
DIVISION	Judgment of People	Judgment of Leadership	Promise of Coming Kingdom	Promise of Coming Captivities	Promise of Coming King	First Plea of God	Second Plea of God	Promise of Final Salvation
TOPIC	Punishment		Promise			Pardon		
	Retribution		Restoration			Repentance		
LOCATION	Judah—Israel							
TIME	c. 735–710 B.C.							

The Book of
MICAH

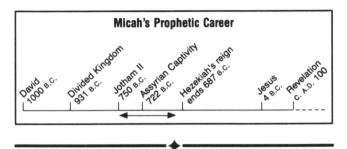

Micah's Prophetic Career

David 1000 B.C. — Divided Kingdom 931 B.C. — Jotham II 750 B.C. — Assyrian Captivity 722 B.C. — Hezekiah's reign ends 687 B.C. — Jesus 4 B.C. — Revelation C. A.D. 100

◆

LANDMARKS OF MICAH

Key Word: *The Judgment and Restoration of Judah*

Micah exposes the injustice of Judah and the righteousness and justice of God. About one-third of the book indicts Israel and Judah for specific sins. Another third of Micah predicts the judgment that will come as a result of those sins. The remaining third of the book is a message of hope and consolation. God's justice will triumph and the divine Deliverer will come.

Key Verses: *Micah 6:8; 7:18*

Key Chapters: *Micah 6; 7*

The closing section of Micah describes a courtroom scene. God has a controversy against His people, and He calls the mountains and hills together to form the jury as He sets forth His case. There can only be one verdict: guilty.

Nevertheless, the book closes on a note of hope. The same God who executes judgment also delights to extend mercy (7:18–20).

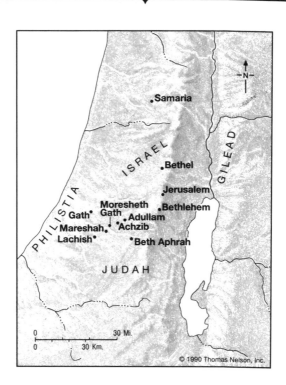

The Assyrian Threat
Geographical Puns in Micah 1:10–14
(See map p. 174.)

The prophet employs a series of clever word plays in announcing the judgment of God to fall upon Judah by means of the invading Assyrian army.

James Moffatt's *The Bible: A New Translation* translates the Hebrew word plays into English quite successfully:

> Weep tears at Teartown (Bochim),
> grovel in the dust at Dustown
>   (Beth Aphrah),
> fare forth stripped, O Fairtown
>   (Saphir)!
> Stirtown (Zaanan) dare not stir,
> Beth-êsel. . . .
> and Maroth hopes in vain;
> for doom descends from the Eternal
> to the very gates of Jerusalem.
>
> To horse and drive away,
>   O Horse town (Lachish),
> O source of Sion's sin,
> where the crimes of Israel centre!
> O maiden Sion, you must part with
> Moresheth of Gath;
> and Israel's kings are ever balked
> at Balkton (Achzib).

Overview of Nahum

FOCUS	Destruction of Nineveh Decreed		Destruction of Nineveh Described		Destruction of Nineveh Deserved	
REFERENCE	1:1 ——————— 1:9 ———————		2:1 ——————— 2:3 ———————		3:1 ——————— 3:12 ——————— 3:19	
DIVISION	General Principles of Divine Judgment	Destruction of Nineveh and Deliverance of Judah	The Call to Battle	Description of the Destruction of Nineveh	Reasons for the Destruction of Nineveh	Inevitable Destruction of Nineveh
TOPIC	Verdict of Vengeance		Vision of Vengeance		Vindication of Vengeance	
	What God Will Do		How God Will Do It		Why God Will Do It	
LOCATION	In Judah Against Nineveh, Capital of Assyria					
TIME	c. 612 B.C.					

The Book of NAHUM

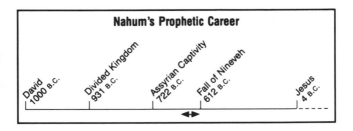

Nahum's Prophetic Career

David 1000 B.C.

Divided Kingdom 931 B.C.

Assyrian Captivity 722 B.C.

Fall of Nineveh 612 B.C.

Jesus 4 B.C.

◆

LANDMARKS OF NAHUM

Key Word: *The Judgment of Nineveh*

If ever a city deserved the title "Here to Stay," Nineveh was that city. But Nahum declares that Nineveh will fall.

Key Verses: *Nahum 1:7, 8; 3:5–7*

Key Chapter: *Nahum 1*

Nahum 1:2–8 portrays the patience, power, holiness, and justice of the living God. He is slow to wrath, but God settles His accounts in full. This book concerns the downfall of Assyria, but it is written for the benefit of the surviving kingdom of Judah.

◆

Overview of Habakkuk

FOCUS	Problems of Habakkuk			Praise of Habakkuk
REFERENCE	1:1 ———— 1:5 ————	1:12 ————	2:2 ————	3:1 ———— 3:19
DIVISION	First Problem of Habakkuk	First Reply of God	Second Problem of Habakkuk	Second Reply of God	Prayer of Praise of Habakkuk
TOPIC	Faith Troubled				Faith Triumphant
	What God Is Doing				Who God Is
LOCATION	The Nation of Judah				
TIME	c. 607 B.C.				

The Book of
HABAKKUK

Habakkuk's Prophetic Career

David 1000 B.C. — Divided Kingdom 931 B.C. — Babylonian Captivity 605 B.C. — Fall of Jerusalem 587 B.C. — Jesus 4 B.C.

LANDMARKS OF HABAKKUK

Key Word: *"The Just Shall Live by His Faith"*

Habakkuk struggles in his faith when he sees men flagrantly violate God's law and distort justice on every level, without fear of divine intervention. He wants to know why God allows this growing iniquity to go unpunished. God's answer satisfies Habakkuk that he can trust Him even in the worst of circumstances because of His matchless wisdom, goodness, and power.

Key Verses: *Habakkuk 2:4; 3:17–19*

Key Chapter: *Habakkuk 3*

The Book of Habakkuk builds to a triumphant climax reached in the last three verses (3:17–19). The beginning of the book and the ending stand in stark contrast: mystery to certainty, questioning to affirming, and complaint to confidence.

◆

Living by Faith
(Habakkuk)

In what seems to be merely an incidental contrast between the arrogance of the Babylonians and the humble submission of the righteousness to God, Habakkuk states a fundamental principle of the gospel: "the just shall live by his faith." When Paul (Rom. 1:17; Gal. 3:11) and the writer of Hebrews (Heb. 10:38) quote this verse, they merely apply the principle laid down by the prophet regarding the importance of faith in man's relationship to God.

The prophets response to the difficult questions put to him: The just shall live by faith.

Question 1: Why does God not respond to the wrong and injustice in the land (1:2–4)?

Answer: He is about to respond by using Babylon as a tool of judgment (1:5–11).

Question 2: Why does God use the wicked Babylonians to punish those more righteous than themselves (1:12, 13)?

Answer: God has chosen this plan of action (2:2, 3). The just person will live by faith in God (2:4). Woe to the unrighteous (2:6–20).

The Book of
ZEPHANIAH

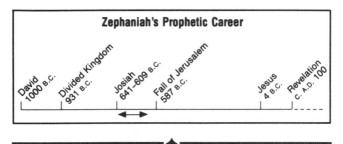

Zephaniah's Prophetic Career

David 1000 B.C. | Divided Kingdom 931 B.C. | Josiah 641–609 B.C. | Fall of Jerusalem 587 B.C. | Jesus 4 B.C. | Revelation C. A.D. 100

LANDMARKS OF ZEPHANIAH

Key Word: *The Day of the Lord*

God is holy and must vindicate His righteousness by calling all the nations of the world into account before Him. The sovereign God will judge not only His own people but also the whole world. Wrath and mercy, severity and kindness, cannot be separated in the character of God.

Key Verses: *Zephaniah 1:14, 15; 2:3*

Key Chapter: *Zephaniah 3*

The last chapter of Zephaniah records the two distinct parts of the day of the Lord: judgment and restoration. Following the conversion of the nation, Israel finally is fully restored. Under the righteous rule of God, Israel fully inherits the blessings contained in the biblical covenants.

Overview of Zephaniah

FOCUS	Judgment in the Day of the Lord				Salvation in the Day of the Lord	
REFERENCE	1:1 ————	1:4 ————	2:4 ————	3:1 ————	3:8 ———— 3:9 ————	3:14 ———— 3:20
DIVISION	Judgment on the Whole Earth	Judgment on the Nation of Judah	Judgment on the Nations Surrounding Judah	Judgment on the City of Jerusalem	Judgment on the Whole Earth	Promise of Conversion	Promise of Restoration
TOPIC	Day of Wrath				Day of Joy	
	Judgment on Judah				Restoration for Judah	
LOCATION	Judah and the Nations					
TIME	c. 630 B.C.					

The Book of HAGGAI

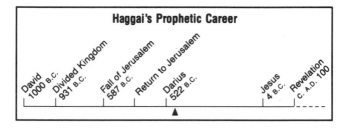

Haggai's Prophetic Career

David 1000 B.C. Divided Kingdom 931 B.C. Fall of Jerusalem 587 B.C. Return to Jerusalem Darius 522 B.C. Jesus 4 B.C. Revelation C. A.D. 100

LANDMARKS OF HAGGAI

Key Word: *The Reconstruction of the Temple*

Haggai's basic theme is clear: the remnant must reorder its priorities and complete the temple before it can expect the blessing of God upon its efforts.

Key Verses: *Haggai 1:7, 8; 2:7–9*

Key Chapter: *Haggai 2*

Verses 6–9 record some of the most startling prophecies in Scripture: "I will shake heaven and earth, the sea and dry land" (the Tribulation) and "they shall come to the Desire of All Nations" and "in this place I will give peace" (the second coming of the Messiah).

Overview of Haggai

FOCUS	Completion of the Latter Temple	Glory of the Latter Temple	Present Blessings of Obedience	Future Blessings Through Promise
REFERENCE	1:1 ———————	2:1 ———————	2:10 ———————	2:20 ——————— 2:23
DIVISION	"Consider Your Ways . . . My House That Is in Ruins."	"The Glory of This Latter Temple Shall Be Greater."	"From This Day I Will Bless You."	"I Will Shake Heaven and Earth."
TOPIC	The Temple of God		The Blessings of God	
	First Rebuke (Present)	First Encouragement (Future)	Second Rebuke (Present)	Second Encouragement (Future)
LOCATION	Jerusalem			
TIME	September 1 520 B.C.	October 21 520 B.C.	December 24 520 B.C.	December 24 520 B.C.

The Temples of the Scriptures
(Haggai)

The Book of Haggai consists of four brief sermons urging the people to re-establish proper priorities and to complete construction of the temple under Zerubbabel. The various temples of the Bible and their significance are described below:

(1) *Solomon's Temple.* The construction of this temple by Solomon was a fulfillment of David's desire to build a "house for the LORD"—a desire which he was never to realize in his lifetime (2 Sam. 7:1–29). The temple was built after the death of David and dedicated by his son (1 Kin. 8:1ff). This temple was destroyed by the armies of Nebuchadnezzar at the fall of Jerusalem in 586 B.C. (Jer. 32:28–44).

(2) *Zerubbabel's Temple.* This is the one under construction during the ministry of the prophet Zechariah. It was completed and dedicated in 516 B. C. (Ezra 6:1–22). It was constructed under the direction of Zerubbabel (Ezra 3:1–8; 4:1–14) who was a descendant of David (1 Chr. 3:19). This temple was desecrated in 169 B.C. by Antiochus Epiphanes.

(3) *Herod's Temple.* Restoration of Zerubbabel's temple began in 19 B.C. under the administration of Herod the Great. The temple was nearing completion in A.D. 70, after nearly 90 years of renovation and enlargement, when it was destroyed by the Romans. Since this time there has been no temple in Jerusalem.

(4) *The Present Temple.* There is a temple in which the Lord reigns at present. According to 1 Cor. 6:19 and 2 Cor. 6:16–18 the present temple of the Lord is the

heart of the believer. There the Lord reigns until the day when the Messiah will return and set up His earthly kingdom and the millennial temple.

(5) *The Temple of Revelation 11.* This temple will be constructed during the Tribulation by the Antichrist. It is mentioned in 2 Thess. 2:4 as the site for the abomination of desolation mentioned by Daniel the prophet (Dan. 9:2) and Jesus (Matt. 24:15). This temple will be destroyed with the kingdom of the Antichrist (see Rev. 17; 18).

(6) *The Millennial Temple.* This is the temple that is described in detail in Ezek. 40:1—42:20. It is this temple that the prophet Zechariah has n view in 6:12, 13. It will be built by the Messiah Himself, who will rule in it as the righteous Priest-King of His own millennial kingdom (6:13).

(7) *The Eternal Temple of His Presence.* This temple is presented in Rev. 21:22. John says there will be no physical temple in the eternal kingdom because ". . . the Lord God Almighty and the Lamb are its temple." This temple will be the greatest of all and it will be the focus of the eternal kingdom as it is presented in Rev. 21:22.

The Book of
ZECHARIAH

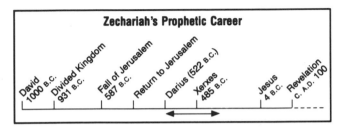

Zechariah's Prophetic Career

David 1000 B.C. | Divided Kingdom 931 B.C. | Fall of Jerusalem 587 B.C. | Return to Jerusalem | Darius (522 B.C.) | Xerxes 485 B.C. | Jesus 4 B.C. | Revelation c. A.D. 100

LANDMARKS OF ZECHARIAH

Key Word: *Prepare for the Messiah*

The first eight chapters frequently allude to the Temple and encourage the people to complete their great work on the new sanctuary. As they build the Temple, they are building their future, because that very structure will be used by the Messiah when He comes to bring salvation.

Key Verses: *Zechariah 8:3; 9:9*

Key Chapter: *Zechariah 14*

Zechariah builds to a tremendous climax in the fourteenth chapter, where he discloses the last siege of Jerusalem and the ultimate holiness of Jerusalem and her people.

Overview of Zechariah

FOCUS	Eight Visions			Four Messages	Two Burdens	
REFERENCE	1:1 ———	1:7 ———	6:9 ———	7:1 ———	9:1 ———	12:1 ——— 14:21
DIVISION	Call to Repentance	Eight Visions	Crowning of Joshua	Question of Fasting	First Burden: Rejection of the Messiah	Second Burden: Reign of the Messiah
TOPIC	Pictures			Problem	Prediction	
	Israel's Fortune			Israel's Fastings	Israel's Future	
LOCATION	Jerusalem					
TIME	While Building the Temple (520–518 B.C.)				After Building the Temple (c. 480–470 B.C.)	

Zechariah's Visions

The visions of Zechariah had historical meaning for his day, but they also have meaning for all time. God will save His people and bring judgment on the wicked.

Vision	Significance
Man and horses among the myrtle trees (1:8)	The Lord will again be merciful to Jerusalem (1:14, 16, 17).
Four horns, four craftsmen (1:18–20)	Those who scattered Judah are cast out (1:21).
Man with measuring line (2:1)	God will be a protective wall of fire around Jerusalem (2:3–5).
Cleansing of Joshua (3:4)	The Servant, the Branch, comes to save (3:8, 9).
Golden lampstand and olive trees (4:2, 3)	The Lord empowers Israel by His Spirit (4:6).
Flying scroll (5:1)	Dishonestly is cursed (5:3).
Woman in the basket (5:6, 7)	Wickedness will be removed (5:9).
Four chariots (6:1)	The spirits of heaven execute judgment on the whole earth (6:5, 7).

Overview of Malachi

FOCUS	Privilege of the Nation	Pollution of the Nation		Promise to the Nation		
REFERENCE	1:1 ———————	1:6 ———————	2:10 ———————	3:16 ———————	4:1 ———	4:4 ——— 4:6
DIVISION	Love of God for the Nation	Sin of the Priests	Sin of the People	Book of Remembrance	Coming of Christ	Coming of Elijah
TOPIC	Past	Present		Future		
	Care of God	Complaint of God		Coming of God		
LOCATION	Jerusalem					
TIME	c. 450 B.C.					

The Book of
MALACHI

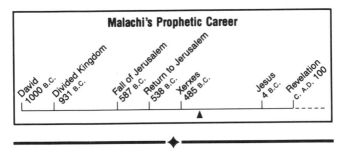

Malachi's Prophetic Career

David 1000 B.C. — Divided Kingdom 931 B.C. — Fall of Jerusalem 587 B.C. — Return to Jerusalem 538 B.C. — Xerxes 485 B.C. — Jesus 4 B.C. — Revelation c. A.D. 100

---◆---

LANDMARKS OF MALACHI

Key Word: *An Appeal to Backsliders*

The divine dialogue in Malachi's prophecy is designed as an appeal to break through the barrier of Israel's disbelief, disappointment, and discouragement. God reveals His continuing love in spite of Israel's lethargy. His appeal in this oracle is for the people and priests to stop and realize that their lack of blessing is not caused by God's lack of concern, but by their disobedience of the covenant law.

Key Verses: *Malachi 2:17—3:1; 4:5, 6*

Key Chapter: *Malachi 3*

The last book of the Old Testament concludes with a dramatic prophecy of the coming of the Messiah and John the Baptist: "I send My messenger, and he will prepare the way before Me" (3:1).

---◆---

The Coming of Christ
(Malachi 3—4)

In four short chapters, the prophet foretells of three important messengers—the priest of the Lord (2:2); John the Baptist (3:1a); and Jesus (3:16). This chart highlights the coming of Jesus—both as prophesied by Malachi and as confirmed in the New Testament:

Malachi's Prophecy	Confirmed in the New Testament
As Messenger of the covenant, Christ comes to His temple (3:1) and purifies His people (3:3).	Christ cleanses the temple (John 2:14–17) and sanctifies His people (Heb. 13:12).
His coming brings judgment (4:1).	Those whose names are not in the Book of Life are cast into the lake of fire (Rev. 20:11–15).
As the Sun of Righteousness, Christ heals His people (4:2)	Christ heals the multitudes; ultimately all sickness will pass away (Matt. 12:15; Rev. 21:4).
His forerunner prepares for the coming of the Lord (3:1; 4:5).	John the Baptist announces Christ (Matt. 11:10–14).

SIX

INTERTESTAMENTAL PERIOD

◆

Bridging the Testaments

The map on p. 194 shows Palestine as a subject region within four successive world empires, beginning with the Assyrian Empire in 750 B.C. and concluding with Alexander's Greek Empire of 331–146 B.C. After his death in 323 B.C., Alexander's leading generals divided the empire and established their own dynasties. Two of these controlled Palestine: first the kingdom of Ptolemy, which held Palestine from 323 B.C. until 198 B.C. when, by battle, it was lost to the kingdom of Seleucus. Then the Syrian Seleucids ruled until the strengthening revolt of the Jewish Hasmonean family (later called the Maccabees) gained complete independence in 143 B.C. Jewish independence of Judea lasted until the Romans occupied the region under general Pompey in 63 B.C. The Romans continued to occupy the whole of Palestine throughout all of New Testament history. Maps illustrating these shifts of political power over Palestine may be found on pages 195, 196, and 197.

Succession of Four World Empires
(750–146 B.C.)

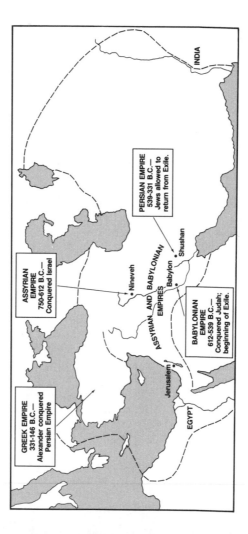

GREEK EMPIRE
331-146 B.C.—
Alexander conquered
Persian Empire

ASSYRIAN
EMPIRE
750-612 B.C.—
Conquered Israel

PERSIAN EMPIRE
539-331 B.C.—
Jews allowed to
return from Exile.

BABYLONIAN
EMPIRE
612-539 B.C.—
Conquered Judah;
beginning of Exile.

ASSYRIAN AND BABYLONIAN
EMPIRES

INDIA

Nineveh

Shushan

Babylon

Jerusalem

EGYPT

Ptolemaic Control of Palestine

(270 B.C.)

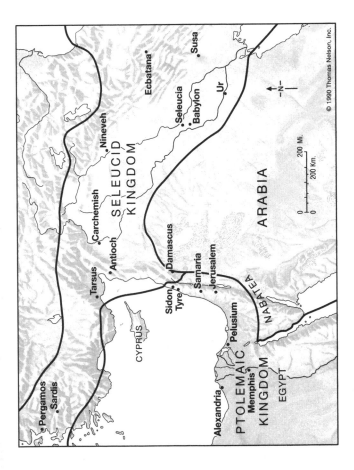

Seleucid Control of Palestine

(c. 190 B.C.)

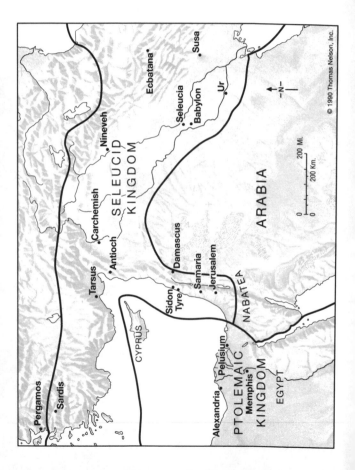

Roman Control of Palestine

(63 B.C.—beyond N.T. times)

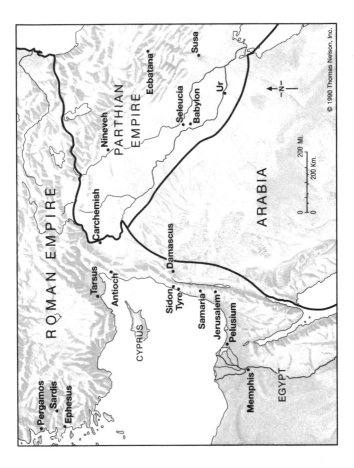

Expansion of Palestine Under the Maccabees

(166–76 B.C.)

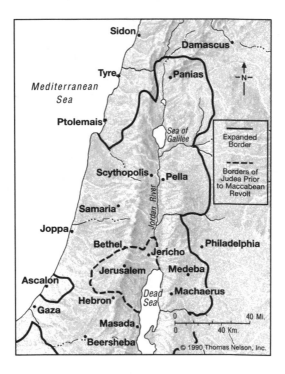

Sidon

Damascus

Tyre

Panias

Mediterranean Sea

Ptolemais

Sea of Galilee

Expanded Border
Borders of Judea Prior to Maccabean Revolt

Scythopolis

Pella

Jordan River

Samaria

Joppa

Bethel

Philadelphia

Jericho

Jerusalem

Medeba

Ascalon

Dead Sea

Machaerus

Hebron

Gaza

Masada

Beersheba

0   40 Mi.

0   40 Km.

PART TWO

◆

THE NEW TESTAMENT

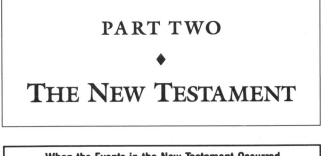

When the Events in the New Testament Occurred

Ezra 500 B.C. | Persian rule 539–352 B.C. | Ptolemies 332–198 B.C. | Seleucids 198–164 B.C. —Revolt | Maccabees | Herod the Great | Birth of Jesus 4 B.C. | Crucifixion Pentecost A.D. 30 | Revelation C. A.D. 100

(not including prophecy unfulfilled when these books were written)

SEVEN

THE GOSPELS AND ACTS

◆

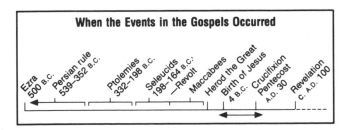

When the Events in the Gospels Occurred

Ezra 500 B.C. | Persian rule 539–352 B.C. | Ptolemies 332–198 B.C. | Seleucids 198–164 B.C. —Revolt | Maccabees | Herod the Great | Birth of Jesus | Crucifixion Pentecost A.D. 30 | Revelation C. A.D. 100

The World of the New Testament

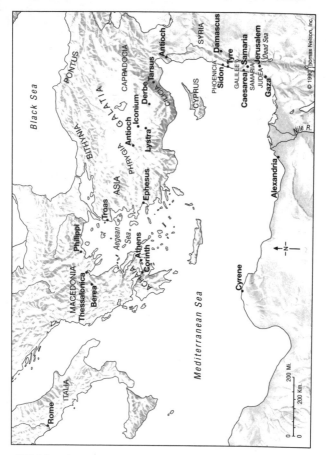

Within sixty years after the death and resurrection of Jesus Christ, the gospel about Him had reached nearly every major area with coasts on the Mediterranean Sea.

Palestine at the Time of Christ

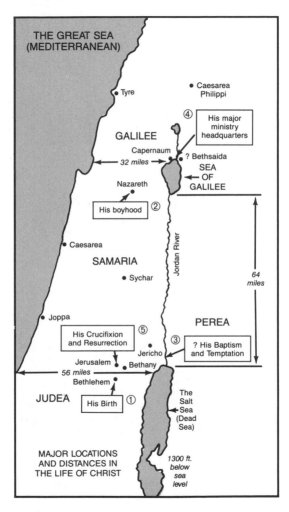

THE GREAT SEA (MEDITERRANEAN)

Tyre

Caesarea Philippi

GALILEE

④ His major ministry headquarters

Capernaum

← 32 miles →

? Bethsaida

SEA OF GALILEE ←

Nazareth

② His boyhood

Caesarea

SAMARIA

Sychar

Jordan River

64 miles

Joppa

PEREA

⑤ His Crucifixion and Resurrection

③ ? His Baptism and Temptation

Jericho

Jerusalem

Bethany

← 56 miles →

Bethlehem

JUDEA

① His Birth

The Salt Sea (Dead Sea)

MAJOR LOCATIONS AND DISTANCES IN THE LIFE OF CHRIST

1300 ft. below sea level

The Gospels Compared and Contrasted

Topics	The Synoptic Gospels			John
	Matthew	Mark	Luke	
Probable Date	A.D. 58-68	A.D. 55-65	A.D. 60-68	A.D. 80-90
Place of Writing	Syria Antioch or Palestine	Rome	Rome/Greece	Ephesus
Original Audience	Jewish mind (Religious)	Roman mind (Pragmatic)	Greek mind (Idealistic)	Universal
Theme	Messiah-King	Servant-Redeemer	Perfect Man	Son of God
Traditional Picture of Christ (cf. Ezek. 1:10; Rev. 4:6-8)	The Lion (strength, authority)	The Bull (service, power)	The Man (wisdom, character)	The Eagle (deity, person)
Portrait of Christ	God-man	God-man		God-man
Perspective	Historical	Historical		Theological
Unique Material	Less unique (Matthew, 42%; Mark, 7%; Luke, 59%)			More unique (92%)
Chronology	Only one Passover mentioned			Three of four Passovers mentioned
Geography	Concentrates on Galilean ministry			Concentrates on Judean ministry
Discourse Material	More public			More private
Teaching Method	Parables			Allegories
Teaching Emphasis	More on ethical, practical teachings			More on the person of Christ
Relationship to Other Gospels	Complementary			Supplementary

Summary of the Life of Christ

Events	Matthew	Mark	Luke	John
1. The Thirty Years of Preparation	1:1–4:11	1:1–13	1:1–4:13	1:19–2:12
2. Early Judean Ministry (about a year)				2:13–4:54
3. The Galilean Ministry: Early Period (from imprisonment of John the Baptist to choosing of the twelve, about four months)	4:12–17 9:1–17 12:1–21	1:14–3:12	4:14–6:11	
4. The Galilean Ministry: Middle Period (from choosing the twelve to withdrawal into northern Galilee; about ten months)	4:18–8:34 9:18–11:30 13:1–15:20	3:13–7:23	6:12–9:17	6:1–70
5. Galilean Ministry: Later Period (from journey into northern Galilee to departure for Jerusalem; about six months)	15:21–18:35	7:24–9:50	9:18–50	7:1–9
6. The Later Judean Ministry (about three months)	19:1, 2		9:51–13:21	7:10–10:42
7. The Perean Ministry (about three months)	19:3–20:34	10:1–52	13:22–19:28	11:1–12:11
8. The Passion Week	21:1–27:66	11:1–15:47	19:29–23:56	12:12–19:42
9. The Resurrection and Post-Resurrection Ministry	28:1–20	10:1–20	24:1–53	20:1–21:25

Overview of the Gospel According to Matthew

FOCUS	Offer of the King			Rejection of the King			
REFERENCE	1:1 ——— 4:12 ———	8:1 ———	11:2 ———	16:13 ———	20:29 ———	28:1 — 28:20	
DIVISION	Presentation of the King	Proclamation of the King	Power of the King	Progressive Rejection of the King	Preparation of the King's Disciples	Presentation and Rejection of the King	Proof of the King
TOPIC		Teaching the Throngs			Teaching the Twelve		
	Chronological	Thematic			Chronological		
LOCATION	Bethlehem and Nazareth	Galilee			Judea		
TIME	c. 4 B.C.—A.D. 30 or 33						

The Gospel According to MATTHEW

◆

LANDMARKS OF MATTHEW

Key Word: *Jesus the King*

By quoting repeatedly from the Old Testament, Matthew validates Christ's claim that He is, in fact, the prophesied Messiah (the Anointed One) of Israel.

Key Verses: *Matthew 16:16–19 and 28:18–20*

Key Chapter: *Matthew 12*

The turning point of Matthew comes in the twelfth chapter when the Pharisees, acting as the leadership of the nation of Israel, formally reject Jesus Christ as the Messiah. Christ's ministry changes immediately with His new teaching of parables, increased attention given to His disciples, and His repeated statement that His death is now near.

◆

Prophecies of the Messiah Fulfilled in Jesus Christ

Prophetic Scripture	Subject	Fulfilled
Genesis 12:3	descendant of Abraham	Matt. 1:1; Luke 3:34
Genesis 17:19	descendant of Isaac	Matt. 1:2; Luke 3:34

Prophetic Scripture	Subject	Fulfilled
Numbers 24:17	descendant of Jacob	Matt. 1:2; Luke 3:34
Hosea 11:1	flight to Egypt	Matt. 2:14, 15
Jeremiah 31:15	slaughter of children	Matt. 2:16–18
Psalm 2:7	declared the Son of God	Matt. 3:17
Isaiah 9:1, 2	Galilean ministry	Matt. 4:13–16
Malachi 4:5, 6	preceded by Elijah	Matt. 11:13, 14
Psalm 78:2–4	speaks in parables	Matt. 13:34
Psalm 8:2	adored by infants	Matt. 21:15, 16
Zechariah 11:12	betrayed for thirty pieces of silver	Matt. 26:14, 15
Isaiah 50:6	spat on and struck	Matt. 26:67
Psalm 22:17, 18	soldiers gambled for His clothing	Matt. 27:35, 36
Psalm 22:1	forsaken by God	Matt. 27:46
Isaiah 53:9	buried with the rich	Matt. 27:57–60
Zechariah 9:9	triumphal entry	Mark 11:7, 9, 11
Psalm 35:11	accused by false witnesses	Mark 14:57, 58
Isaiah 53:7	silent to accusations	Mark 15:4, 5
Isaiah 53:12	crucified with malefactors	Mark 15:27, 28
Psalm 16:10; 49:15	to be resurrected	Mark 16:6, 7

Prophetic Scripture	Subject	Fulfilled
Psalm 68:18	His ascension to God's right hand	Mark 16:19; 1 Cor. 15:4; Eph. 4:8
Isaiah 7:14	to be born of a virgin	Luke 1:26, 27, 30, 31
Isaiah 9:7	heir to the throne of David	Luke 1:32, 33
Daniel 9:25	time for His birth	Luke 2:1, 2
Micah 5:2	born in Bethlehem	Luke 2:4, 5, 7
Isaiah 40:3–5	the way prepared	Luke 3:3–6
Genesis 49:10	from the tribe of Judah	Luke 3:33
Isaiah 61:1, 2	to bind up the brokenhearted	Luke 4:18
Malachi 3:1	preceded by a forerunner	Luke 7:24, 27
Psalm 41:9	betrayed by a close friend	Luke 22:47, 48
Isaiah 53:3	rejected by His own people, the Jews	John 1:11; Luke 23:18
Psalm 109:4	prayer for His enemies	Luke 23:34
Psalm 22:7, 8	sneered and mocked	Luke 23:35
Isaiah 53:1	not believed	John 12:37, 38
Psalm 35:19	hated without reason	John 15:24, 25
Psalm 34:20	no bones broken	John 19:32, 33, 36

Prophetic Scripture	Subject	Fulfilled
Zechariah 12:10	His side pierced	John 19:34
Zechariah 12:10	pierced through hands and feet	John 20:27
Deuteronomy 18:15	a prophet	Acts 3:20, 22
Psalm 69:9	was reproached	Rom. 15:3
Isaiah 53:5	vicarious sacrifice	Rom. 5:6, 8
Genesis 3:15	seed of a woman	Gal. 4:4
Psalm 45:6; 102:25–27	anointed and eternal	Heb. 1:8–12
Psalm 110:4	priest after order of Melchizedek	Heb. 5:5, 6

Herod's Kingdom at Jesus' Birth

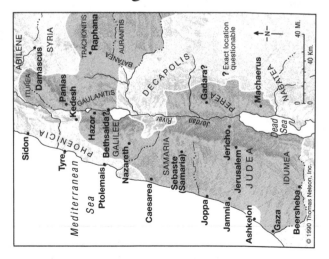

Family Tree of Herod

Herod was the family name of several Roman rulers who served as provincial governors of Palestine and surrounding regions during New Testament times. This family tree can help you sort out the Herods you encounter in the Gospels and Acts.

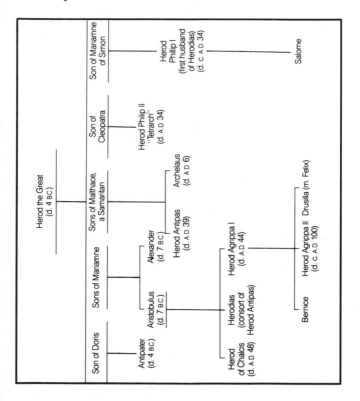

New Testament Political Rulers

Roman Emperor	Rulers of Palestine		
	Herod the Great (37–4 B.C.)		
	Judea	Galilee and Perea	Other Provinces
Augustus Caesar (31 B.C.–A.D. 14)	Archelaus (4 B.C.–A.D. 6) Coponius (A.D. 6–8) Ambivius (A.D. 9–12) Annius Rufus (A.D. 12–15) Valerius Gratus (A.D. 15–26) Pontius Pilate (A.D. 26–36) Marcellus (A.D. 37)	Herod Antipas (4 B.C.–A.D. 39)	Herod Philip II (4 B.C.–A.D. 34)
Tiberius Caesar (A.D. 14–37)			
Caligula (A.D. 37–41)			

Roman Emperors	Judean Rulers	
Claudius (A.D. 41–54)	Herod Agrippa I (A.D. 37–44) Cuspius Fadus (A.D. 44–46) Tiberius Alexander (A.D. 46–48) Ventidius Cumanus (A.D. 48–52) M. Antonius Felix (A.D. 52–60) Porcius Festus (A.D. 60–62) Clodius Albinus (A.D. 62–64) Gessius Florus (A.D. 64–66)	Herod Agrippa II (Began to rule in A.D. 34 in other provinces and in A.D. 39 in Galilee and Perea.)
Nero (A.D. 54–68)		
Galba, Otho, Vitellius (A.D. 68–69)	Jewish Revolt (A.D. 66–70)	
Vespasian (A.D. 69–79)		
Titus (A.D. 79–81)		
Domitian (A.D. 81–96)		

Mary, Joseph and Jesus Flee to Egypt
(Matthew 2)

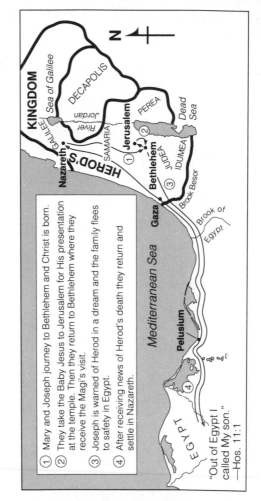

① Mary and Joseph journey to Bethlehem and Christ is born.
② They take the Baby Jesus to Jerusalem for His presentation at the temple. Then they return to Bethlehem where they receive the Magi's visit.
③ Joseph is warned of Herod in a dream and the family flees to safety in Egypt.
④ After receiving news of Herod's death they return and settle in Nazareth.

"Out of Egypt I called My son."
—Hos. 11:1

Baptism, Temptation, and Galilean Ministry

All three Synoptic Gospels record the baptism and temptation of Jesus. This map traces the possible route taken by Jesus to leave Nazareth, go to the site of John's baptisms, and then enter the wilderness of Judea. The map on p. 214 focuses on His subsequent ministry in Galilee.

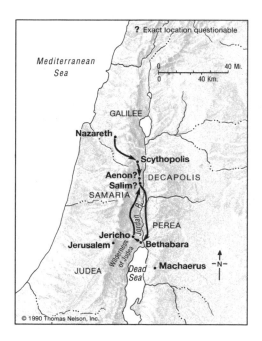

© 1990 Thomas Nelson, Inc.

Galilean Ministry

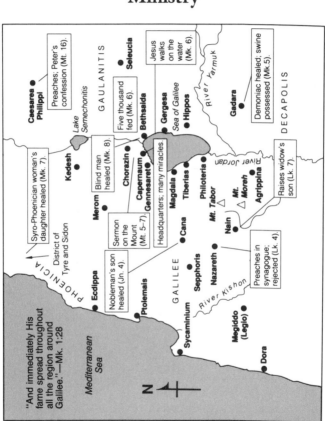

THE PARABLES OF JESUS CHRIST

Parable	Matthew	Mark	Luke
1. Lamp Under a Basket	5:14–16	4:21, 22	8:16, 17 11:33–36
2. A Wise Man Builds on Rock and a Foolish Man Builds on Sand	7:24–27		6:47–49
3. Unshrunk (New) Cloth on an Old Garment	9:16	2:21	5:36
4. New Wine in Old Wineskins	9:17	2:22	5:37, 38
5. The Sower	13:3–23	4:2–20	8:4–15
6. The Tares (Weeds)	13:24–30		
7. The Mustard Seed	13:31, 32	4:30–32	13:18, 19
8. The Leaven	13:33		13:20, 21
9. The Hidden Treasure	13:44		
10. The Pearl of Great Price	13:45, 46		
11. The Dragnet	13:47–50		
12. The Lost Sheep	18:12–14		15:3–7
13. The Unforgiving Servant	18:23–35		
14. The Workers in the Vineyard	20:1–16		
15. The Two Sons	21:28–32		
16. The Wicked Vinedressers	21:33–45	12:1–12	20:9–19
17. The Wedding Feast	22:2–14		
18. The Fig Tree	24:32–44	13:28–32	21:29–33
19. The Wise and Foolish Virgins	25:1–13		
20. The Talents	25:14–30		
21. The Growing Seed		4:26–29	
22. The Absent Householder		13:33–37	
23. The Creditor and Two Debtors			7:41–43
24. The Good Samaritan			10:30–37

PARABLES OF JESUS—*Cont'd*			
Parable	*Matthew*	*Mark*	*Luke*
25. A Friend in Need			11:5–13
26. The Rich Fool			12:16–21
27. The Faithful Servant and the Evil Servant			12:35–40
28. Faithful and Wise Steward			12:42–48
29. The Barren Fig Tree			13:6–9
30. The Great Supper			14:16–24
31. Building a Tower and a King Making War			14:25–35
32. The Lost Coin			15:8–10
33. The Lost Son			15:11–32
34. The Unjust Steward			16:1–13
35. The Rich Man and Lazarus			16:19–31
36. Unprofitable Servants			17:7–10
37. The Persistent Widow			18:1–8
38. The Pharisee and the Tax Collector			18:9–14
39. The Minas (Pounds)			19:11–27

The Rise of Rejection

After Peter made his great confession at Caesarea Philippi (see map p. 214), Jesus returned to Galilee via the Decapolis region, crossing the River Jordan north of the Dead Sea. In the face of rising opposition, He completed His final ministry in Central Palestine (see map p. 217) and set His face for Jerusalem and what we now know as the Passion Week (see pp. 220–221).

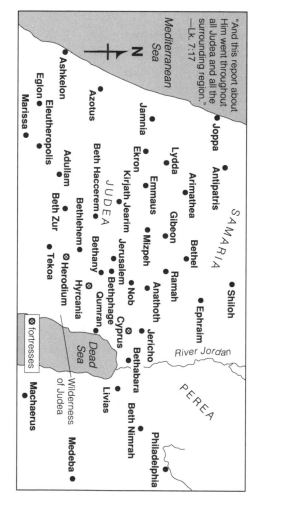

Central Palestine in Christ's Time

"And this report about Him went throughout all Judea and all the surrounding region."
—Lk. 7:17

Christ's Trial, Crucifixion, and Resurrection

The events of Passion Week (see pp. 220–221) occurred in the city of Jerusalem, beginning with Jesus' triumphal entry on Palm Sunday. The accompanying map details the chronology of events. However, after His resurrection, Jesus appeared to His disciples and over five hundred other believers throughout the entire regions of Judea and Galilee, as the map on p. 219 shows.

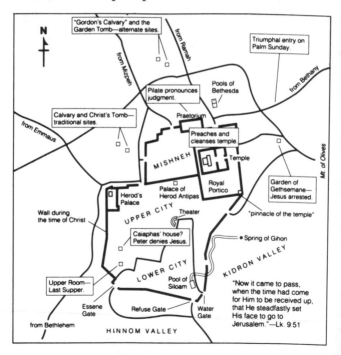

N

"Gordon's Calvary" and the Garden Tomb—alternate sites.

from Ramah

from Mizpeh

Triumphal entry on Palm Sunday.

from Bethany

Pools of Bethesda

Pilate pronounces judgment.

Calvary and Christ's Tomb—traditional sites.

from Emmaus

Praetorium

Preaches and cleanses temple.

MISHNEH

Temple

Palace of Herod Antipas

Royal Portico

Garden of Gethsemane—Jesus arrested.

Herod's Palace

Mt. of Olives

Wall during the time of Christ

UPPER CITY

Theater

"pinnacle of the temple"

Caiaphas' house? Peter denies Jesus.

Spring of Gihon

LOWER CITY

Pool of Siloam

KIDRON VALLEY

Upper Room—Last Supper.

Essene Gate

Refuse Gate

Water Gate

"Now it came to pass, when the time had come for Him to be received up, that He steadfastly set His face to go to Jerusalem."—Lk. 9:51

from Bethlehem

HINNOM VALLEY

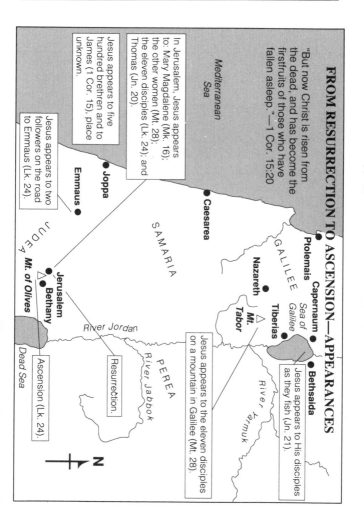

FROM RESURRECTION TO ASCENSION—APPEARANCES

"But now Christ is risen from the dead, and has become the firstfruits of those who have fallen asleep."—1 Cor. 15:20

In Jerusalem, Jesus appears to: Mary Magdalene (Mk. 16); the other women (Mt. 28); the eleven disciples (Lk. 24); and Thomas (Jn. 20).

Jesus appears to five hundred brethren and to James (1 Cor. 15), place unknown.

Jesus appears to two followers on the road to Emmaus (Lk. 24).

Jesus appears to the eleven disciples on a mountain in Galilee (Mt. 28).

Jesus appears to His disciples as they fish (Jn. 21).

Resurrection.

Ascension (Lk. 24).

Mediterranean Sea

Joppa

Emmaus

Caesarea

SAMARIA

JUDEA

Jerusalem

Bethany

Mt. of Olives

River Jordan

Dead Sea

GALILEE

Ptolemais

Capernaum

Bethsaida

Sea of Galilee

Nazareth

Mt. Tabor

Tiberias

PEREA

River Jabbok

River Yarmuk

N

The Passion Week

Day	Event	Biblical Reference
Sunday	The triumphal entry into Jerusalem	Matt. 21:1–11; Mark 11:1–11
Monday	Cleanses the temple in Jerusalem	Matt. 21:12–17; Mark 11:15–19
Tuesday	The Sanhedrin challenges Jesus' authority	Luke 20:1–8
	Jesus foretells the destruction of Jerusalem and His Second Coming	Matt. 24; 25
	Mary anoints Jesus at Bethany	John 12:2–8
	Judas bargains with the Jewish rulers to betray Jesus	Luke 22:3–6
Thursday	Jesus eats the Passover meal with His disciples and institutes the Memorial Supper	Matt. 26:17–30; Mark 14:22–26; John 13:1–30
	Prays in Gethsemane for His disciples	John 17
Friday	His betrayal and arrest in the Garden of Gethsemane	Matt. 26:47–56; Mark 14:43–50
	Jesus questioned by Annas, the former high priest	John 18:12–24
	Condemned by Caiaphas and the Sanhedrin	Mark 14:53–65
	Peter denies Jesus three times	John 18:15–27
	Jesus is formally condemned by the Sanhedrin	Luke 22:66–71
	Judas commits suicide	Matt. 27:3–10

Day	Event	Biblical Reference
	The trial of Jesus before Pilate	Luke 23:1–5
	Jesus' appearance before Herod Antipas	Luke 23:6–12
	Formally sentenced to death by Pilate	Luke 23:13–25
	Jesus is mocked and crucified between two thieves	Mark 15:16–27
	The veil of the temple is torn as Jesus dies	Matt. 27:51–56
	His burial in the tomb of Joseph of Arimathea	John 19:31–42
Sunday	Jesus is raised from the dead	Matt. 28:1–15; Luke 24:1–9

The Gospel According to MARK

◆

LANDMARKS OF MARK

Key Word: *Jesus the Servant*

Mark's theme is captured well in 10:45 because Jesus is portrayed in this book as a Servant and as the Redeemer of men (cf. Phil. 2:5–11). Mark shows his gentile readers how the Son of God—rejected by His own people—achieved ultimate victory through apparent defeat.

Key Verses: *Mark 10:43–45 and 8:34–37*

Overview of the Gospel According to Mark

FOCUS	To Serve			To Sacrifice	
REFERENCE	1:1 ——— 2:13 ———	8:27 ———	11:1 ———	16:1 ———	16:20
DIVISION	Presentation of the Servant	Opposition to the Servant	Instruction by the Servant	Rejection of the Servant	Resurrection of the Servant
TOPIC	Sayings and Signs			Sufferings	
	c. 3 Years		c. 6 Months	8 Days	
LOCATION	Galilee and Perea			Judea and Jerusalem	
TIME	c. A.D. 29–30 or 33				

Key Chapter: *Mark 8*

Mark 8 is a pivotal chapter showing the change of emphasis in Jesus' ministry after Peter's confession, "You are the Christ." After this point Jesus begins to fortify His men for His forthcoming suffering and death.

---◆---

The Gospel of Mark focuses on Jesus Christ as both a man of action and a servant. The accounts of Jesus' miracles begin in Mark in the very first chapter, as the following chart shows:

The Gospel According to LUKE

---◆---

LANDMARKS OF LUKE

Key Word: *Jesus the Son of Man*

Luke portrays Christ in His fullest humanity by devoting more of his writing to Christ's feelings and humanity than any other gospel.

Key Verses: *Luke 1:3, 4 and 19:10*

Key Chapter: *Luke 15*

Captured in the three parables of the Lost Sheep, Lost Coin, and Lost Son is the crux of this gospel: that God through Christ has come to seek and to save that which was lost.

---◆---

THE MIRACLES OF JESUS CHRIST

Miracle	Matthew	Mark	Luke	John
1. Cleansing a Leper	8:2	1:40	5:12	
2. Healing a Centurion's Servant (of paralysis)	8:5		7:1	
3. Healing Peter's Mother-in-law	8:14	1:30	4:38	
4. Healing the Sick at Evening	8:16	1:32	4:40	
5. Stilling the Storm	8:23	4:35	8:22	
6. Demons Entering a Herd of Swine	8:28	5:1	8:26	
7. Healing a Paralytic	9:2	2:3	5:18	
8. Raising the Ruler's Daughter	9:18, 23	5:22, 35	8:40, 49	
9. Healing the Hemorrhaging Woman	9:20	5:25	8:43	
10. Healing Two Blind Men	9:27			
11. Curing a Demon-possessed, Mute Man	9:32			
12. Healing a Man's Withered Hand	12:9	3:1	6:6	
13. Curing a Demon-possessed, Blind and Mute Man	12:22		11:14	
14. Feeding the Five Thousand	14:13	6:30	9:10	6:1
15. Walking on the Sea	14:25	6:48		6:19
16. Healing the Gentile Woman's Daughter	15:21	7:24		
17. Feeding the Four Thousand	15:32	8:1		

MIRACLES OF JESUS—*Cont'd*				
Miracle	*Matthew*	*Mark*	*Luke*	*John*
18. Healing the Epileptic Boy	17:14	9:17	9:38	
19. Temple Tax in the Fish's Mouth	17:24			
20. Healing Two Blind Men	20:30	10:46	18:35	
21. Withering the Fig Tree	21:18	11:12		
22. Casting Out an Unclean Spirit		1:23	4:33	
23. Healing a Deaf Mute		7:31		
24. Healing a Blind Paralytic at Bethsaida		8:22		
25. Escape from the Hostile Multitude			4:30	
26. Draught of Fish			5:1	
27. Raising of a Widow's Son at Nain			7:11	
28. Healing the Infirm, Bent Woman			13:11	
29. Healing the Man with Dropsy			14:1	
30. Cleansing the Ten Lepers			17:11	
31. Restoring a Servant's Ear			22:51	
32. Turning Water into Wine				2:1
33. Healing the Nobleman's Son (of fever)				4:46
34. Healing an Infirm Man at Bethesda				5:1
35. Healing the Man Born Blind				9:1
36. Raising of Lazarus				11:43
37. Second Draught of Fish				21:1

Overview of Luke

FOCUS	Introduction of the Son of Man	Ministry of the Son of Man	Rejection of the Son of Man	Crucifixion and Resurrection of the Son of Man
REFERENCE	1:1 ——————— 4:14 ———————	9:51 ———————	19:28 ———————	24:53
DIVISION	Advent	Activities	Antagonism and Admonition	Application and Authentication
TOPIC	Seeking the Lost			Saving the Lost
	Miracles Prominent		Teaching Prominent	
LOCATION	Israel	Galilee	Israel	Jerusalem
TIME	c. 4 B.C.—A.D. 30 or 33			

New Testament Women

Luke, unlike the other Gospels, opens with the birth of John the Baptist and the story of Zacharias and Elizabeth (Luke 1:5, 13). Luke and Acts are notable for their focus on women, beginning with Elizabeth and Mary, the mother of Jesus. Mary is portrayed as an enduring example of faith, humility, and service (Luke 1:26–56). Other notable women of the New Testament include the following:

Name	Description	Biblical Reference
Anna	Recognized Jesus as the long-awaited Messiah	Luke 2:36–38
Bernice	Sister of Agrippa before whom Paul made his defense	Acts 25:13
Candace	A queen of Ethiopia	Acts 8:27
Chloe	Woman who knew of divisions in the church at Corinth	1 Cor. 1:11
Claudia	Christian of Rome	2 Tim. 4:21
Damaris	Woman of Athens converted under Paul's ministry	Acts 17:34
Dorcas (Tabitha)	Christian in Joppa who was raised from the dead by Peter	Acts 9:36–41
Drusilla	Wife of Felix, governor of Judea	Acts 24:24
Elizabeth	Mother of John the Baptist	Luke 1:5, 13
Eunice	Mother of Timothy	2 Tim. 1:5
Herodias	Queen who demanded the execution of John the Baptist	Matt. 14:3–10
Joanna	Provided for the material needs of Jesus	Luke 8:3

Name	Description	Biblical Reference
Lois	Grandmother of Timothy	2 Tim. 1:5
Lydia	Converted under Paul's ministry in Philippi	Acts 16:14
Martha and Mary	Sisters of Lazarus; friends of Jesus	Luke 10:38–42
Mary Magdalene	Woman from whom Jesus cast out demons	Matt. 27:56–61; Mark 16:9
Phoebe	A servant, perhaps a deaconess, in the church at Cenchrea	Rom. 16:1, 2
Priscilla	Wife of Aquila; laborer with Paul at Corinth and Ephesus	Acts 18:2, 18, 19
Salome	Mother of Jesus' disciples James and John	Matt. 20:20–24
Sapphira	Held back goods from the early Christian community	Acts 5:1
Susanna	Provided for the material needs of Jesus	Luke 8:3

The Savior of the World

Luke contains much in common with the other Synoptic Gospels—Matthew and Mark—but about half of Luke's material is exclusively his own. One distinguishing feature of Luke is his emphasis on the universality of the Christian message. Jesus is not just the Jewish Messiah, but the Savior of the whole world (2:32; 24:27). In presenting Jesus as the Savior of all people, Luke pays particular attention to Jesus' ministry to the poor, the outcasts, and to women (see "New Testament Women," p. 227).

In Luke, Jesus is the ideal Son of Man who identified

with the sorrow and plight of sinful humanity in order to carry our sorrows and accomplish the work of salvation. Jesus alone fulfills the ideal of human perfection. This perfection is particularly demonstrated in Jesus' response to temptation: Where the first Adam failed, Jesus as the second Adam triumphed (see chart below).

Temptation: The Two Adams Contrasted

Both Adam and Christ faced three aspects of temptation. Adam yielded, bringing upon humankind sin and death. Christ resisted, resulting in justification and life.

1 John 2:16	Genesis 3:6 First Adam	Luke 4:1-13 Second Adam—Christ
"the lust of the flesh"	"the tree was good for food"	"command this stone to become bread"
"the lust of the eyes"	"it was pleasant to the eyes"	"the devil . . . showed Him all the kingdoms"
"the pride of life"	"a tree desirable to make one wise"	"throw Yourself down from here"

The Twelve Apostles

The Synoptic Gospels all record the calling of the twelve apostles in a strikingly similar manner. Luke even repeats the list in Acts 1; however, John's Gospel does not contain a listing of the apostles.

Matthew and Mark have the name Thaddaeus, while Luke in his two lists has Judas (of James). Some think

Judas may have been his original name and that it was changed later to Thaddaeus (meaning perhaps "warm-hearted") in order to avoid the stigma attached to the name Judas Iscariot.

It is interesting that all four lists begin with Simon Peter and end with Judas Iscariot (except the Acts 1 list, for Judas had already killed himself). Also, the names would appear to be in groups of four. Peter, Andrew, James, and John are always in the first group—though not always in that order—and Philip, Bartholomew, Thomas, and Matthew are in the second group in all four lists.

In all four lists, Peter's name heads the first group, Philip heads the second, and James (of Alphaeus) heads the third.

Matt. 10:2–4	Mk. 3:16–19	Lk. 6:14–16	Acts 1:13
Simon Peter	Simon Peter	Simon Peter	Simon Peter
Andrew	James	Andrew	John
James	John	James	James
John	Andrew	John	Andrew
Philip	Philip	Philip	Philip
Bartholomew	Bartholomew	Bartholomew	Thomas
Thomas	Matthew	Matthew	Bartholomew
Matthew	Thomas	Thomas	Matthew
James (of Alphaeus)	James (of Alphaeus)	James (of Alphaeus)	James (of Alphaeus)
Thaddaeus	Thaddaeus	Simon (the Zealot)	Simon (the Zealot)
Simon (the Cananite)	Simon (the Cananite)	Judas (of James)	Judas (of James)
Judas Iscariot	Judas Iscariot	Judas Iscariot	. . . .

Titles of Christ

The two most popular titles or names Christians use in speaking of our Lord are *Jesus,* a translation of the Hebrew word *Joshua,* which means "YAHWEH Is Salvation," and *Christ,* a transliteration of the Greek term *Christos,* meaning "Anointed One" or "Messiah." Following are some other significant names or titles for Christ used in the New Testament. Each title expresses a distinct truth about Jesus and His relationship to believers.

Name or Title	Significance	Biblical Reference
Adam, Last Adam	First of the new race of the redeemed	1 Cor. 15:45
Alpha and Omega	The beginning and ending of all things	Rev. 21:6
Bread of Life	The one essential food	John 6:35
Chief Cornerstone	A sure foundation for life	Eph. 2:20
Chief Shepherd	Protector, sustainer, and guide	1 Pet. 5:4
Firstborn from the Dead	Leads us into resurrection and eternal life	Col. 1:18
Good Shepherd	Provider and caretaker	John 10:11
Great Shepherd of the Sheep	Trustworthy guide and protector	Heb. 13:20
High Priest	A perfect sacrifice for our sins	Heb. 3:1
Holy One of God	Sinless in His nature	Mark 1:24
Immanuel (God With Us)	Stands with us in all of life's circumstances	Matt. 1:23
King of Kings, Lord of Lords	The Almighty, before whom every knee will bow	Rev. 19:16

Name or Title	Significance	Biblical Reference
Lamb of God	Gave His life as a sacrifice on our behalf	John 1:29
Light of the World	Brings hope in the midst of darkness	John 9:5
Lord of Glory	The power and presence of the living God	1 Cor. 2:8
Mediator between God and Men	Brings us into God's presence redeemed and forgiven	1 Tim. 2:5
Only Begotten of the Father	The unique, one-of-a-kind Son of God	John 1:14
Prophet	Faithful proclaimer of the truths of God	Acts 3:22
Savior	Delivers from sin and death	Luke 1:47
Seed of Abraham	Mediator of God's covenant	Gal. 3:16
Son of Man	Identifies with us in our humanity	Matt. 18:11
The Word	Present with God at the creation	John 1:1

The Gospel of
JOHN

♦

LANDMARKS OF JOHN

Key Word: *Believe*

The fourth gospel has the clearest statement of purpose in the Bible: "But these are written that you may believe that Jesus is the Christ, the Son of God, and that believing you may have life in His name" (20:31). John selected the signs he used for the specific purpose of creating intellectual ("that you may believe") and spiritual ("that believing you may have life") conviction about the Son of God.

Key Verses: *John 1:11–13 and John 20:30, 31*

Key Chapter: *John 3*

John 3:16 is without doubt the most quoted and preached verse in all of Scripture. Captured in it is the gospel in its clearest and simplest form: that salvation is a gift of God and is obtainable only through belief.

———————————◆———————————

Jesus' High Priestly Prayer

The longest recorded prayer of Jesus, called the "High Priestly Prayer," is found in John 17:1–26. After voicing a triumphiant declaration of victory in 16:33 ("I have overcome the world") Jesus prays:

(1) For Himself (vv. 1–5):
   He affirms the glory of the Cross (vv. 1, 2).
   He expresses the very essence of eternal life (vv. 3, 4).
   He rejoices in the shared glory of the Father (v. 5).

(2) For His disciples (vv. 6–19):
   He prays for their knowledge (vv. 6–9).
   He prays for their perseverance (vv. 10–12).
   He prays for their joy (v. 13).
   He prays for their sanctification (vv. 14–17).
   He prays for their mission (vv. 18, 19).

Overview of John

FOCUS	Incarnation of the Son of God	Presentation of the Son of God	Opposition to the Son of God	Preparation of the Disciples	Crucifixion and Resurrection of the Son of God
REFERENCE	1:1 ———	1:19 ———	5:1 ———	13:1 ———	18:1 ——— 21:25
DIVISION	Introduction to Christ	Revelation of Christ	Rejection of Christ	Revelation of Christ	Rejection of Christ
		Seven Miracles		Upper Room Discourse	Supreme Miracle
TOPIC	That You Might Believe			That You Might Have Life	
LOCATION			Israel		
TIME	A Few Years			A Few Hours	A Few Weeks

(3) For future believers (vv. 20–26):
　He prays for their oneness (vv. 20–22).
　He prays for their perfect unity (v. 23).
　He prays for their future presence with Him (vv. 24, 25).
　He prays for their mutual love (v. 26).

The Death of Jesus

John's Gospel presents Jesus' death as the fulfillment of Old Testament prophecy (18:8, 9) and as an event appointed by His Father (18:11):

Aspect of Jesus' Death	Old Testament Reference
In obedience to His Father (18:11)	Psalm 40:8
Announced by Himself (18:32; see 3:14)	Numbers 21:8, 9
In the place of His people (18:14)	Isaiah 53:4–6
With evildoers (19:18)	Isaiah 53:12
In innocence (19:6)	Isaiah 53:9
Crucified (19:18)	Psalm 22:16
Buried in a rich man's tomb (19:38–42)	Isaiah 53:9

Overview of Acts

FOCUS	Witness in Jerusalem		Witness in Judea and Samaria	Witness to the End of the Earth	
REFERENCE	1:1 ———— 3:1 ————		8:5 ———————— 13:1 ————————		21:17 —— 28:31
DIVISION	Power of the Church	Progress of the Church	Expansion of the Church	Paul's Three Journeys	Paul's Trials
TOPIC	Jews		Samaritans	Gentiles	
	Peter		Philip	Paul	
LOCATION	Jerusalem		Judea and Samaria	Uttermost Part	
TIME	2 or 5 Years (A.D. 30 or 33–35)		13 Years (A.D. 35–48)	14 Years (A.D. 48–62)	

The ACTS *of the Apostles*

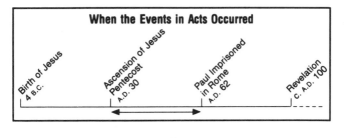

When the Events in Acts Occurred

Birth of Jesus
4 B.C.

Ascension of Jesus
Pentecost
A.D. 30

Paul Imprisoned
in Rome
A.D. 62

Revelation
C. A.D. 100

◆

LANDMARKS OF ACTS

Key Word: *Empowered for Witness*

Because of Luke's strong emphasis on the ministry of the Holy Spirit, this book could be regarded as "The Acts of the Spirit of Christ working in and through the Apostles."

Key Verses: *Acts 1:8 and 2:42–47*

Key Chapter: *Acts 2*

Chapter 2 records the earth-changing events of the Day of Pentecost when the Holy Spirit comes, fulfilling Christ's command to wait until the Holy Spirit arrives to empower and direct the witness. The Spirit transforms a small group of fearful men into a thriving, worldwide church that is ever moving forward and fulfilling the Great Commission.

◆

The Nations of Pentecost

In the first Christian century, Jewish communities were located primarily in the eastern part of the Roman Empire, where Greek was the common language, but also existed as far west as Italy and as far east as Babylonia. In addition to people from the nations shown here, those present on the Day of Pentecost (Acts 2:9–11) included visitors from Mesopotamia and even farther east, from Parthia, Media, and Elam (present-day Iran).

The Work of the Holy Spirit

The New Testament understands the Holy Spirit to be the assurance of the risen Lord Jesus indwelling believers.

In the beginning

- Active and present at creation, hovering over the unordered conditions (Gen. 1:2)

In the Old Testament

- The origin of supernatural abilities (Gen. 41:38)
- The giver of artistic skill (Ex. 31:2–5)
- The source of power and strength (Judg. 3:9, 10)
- The inspiration of prophecy (1 Sam. 19:20, 23)
- The mediation of God's message (Mic. 3:8)

In Old Testament prophecy

- The cleansing of the heart for holy living (Ezek. 36:25–29)

In salvation

- Brings conviction (John 16:8–11)
- Regenerates the believer (Titus 3:5)
- Sanctifies the believer (2 Thess. 2:13)

- Completely indwells the believer (John 14:17; Rom. 8:9–11)

In the New Testament

- Imparts spiritual truth (John 14:26; 16:13; 1 Cor. 2:13–15)
- Glorifies Christ (John 16:14)
- Endows with power for gospel proclamation (Acts 1:8)
- Fills believers (Acts 2:4)
- Pours out God's love in the heart (Rom. 5:5)
- Enables believers to walk in holiness (Rom. 8:1–8; Gal. 5:16–25)
- Makes intercession (Rom. 8:26)
- Imparts gifts for ministry (1 Cor. 12:4–11)
- Strengthens the inner being (Eph. 3:16)

In the written Word

- Inspired the writing of Scripture (2 Tim. 3:16; 2 Pet. 1:21)

Major Sermons in Acts

Several important sermons and speeches are recorded in the Book of Acts. Over twenty are included, with the majority coming from Peter (7 total) and Paul (11 total). The chart (opposite page) lists the more significant, together with the theme and text location.

New Testament Deliverances

In New Testament times Christian believers were often delivered from grim circumstances through a miraculous

Major Sermons in Acts

Speech	Theme	Reference
Peter to crowds at Pentecost	Peter's explanation of the meaning of Pentecost	Acts 2:14-40
Peter to crowds at the temple	The Jewish people should repent for crucifying the Messiah	Acts 3:12-26
Peter to the Sanhedrin	Testimony that a helpless man was healed by the power of Jesus	Acts 4:5-12
Stephen to the Sanhedrin	Stephen's rehearsal of Jewish history, accusing the Jews of killing the Messiah	Acts 7
Peter to Gentiles	Gentiles can be saved in the same manner as Jews	Acts 10:28-47
Peter to church at Jerusalem	Peter's testimony of his experiences at Joppa and a defense of his ministry to the Gentiles	Acts 11:4-18
Paul to synagogue at Antioch	Jesus was the Messiah in fulfillment of Old Testament prophecies	Acts 13:16-41
Peter to Jerusalem council	Salvation by grace available to all	Acts 15:7-11
James to Jerusalem council	Gentile converts do not require circumcision	Acts 15:13-21
Paul to Ephesian elders	Remain faithful in spite of false teachers and persecution	Acts 20:17-35
Paul to crowd at Jerusalem	Paul's statement of his conversion and his mission to the Gentiles	Acts 22:1-21
Paul to Sanhedrin	Paul's defense, declaring himself a Pharisee and a Roman citizen	Acts 23:1-6
Paul to King Agrippa	Paul's statement of his conversion and his zeal for the gospel	Acts 26
Paul to Jewish leaders at Rome	Paul's statement about his Jewish heritage	Acts 28:17-20

display of God's power. Paul and Silas, for example, were
beaten and imprisoned as troublemakers because of their
preaching in Philippi. While they prayed and sang during the night, the prison was shaken by an earthquake
and they were released to continue their work (Acts
16:16–40).

Here are several other specific instances of God's miraculous deliverance of people of faith in New Testament
times:

Name	God's Action	Biblical References
Gadarene with unclean spirit	Delivered from demon possession by Jesus	Mark 5:1–15
Boy with an unclean spirit		Mark 9:14–29
Lazarus	Raised from the dead by Jesus	John 11:38–44
Jesus	Raised from the dead after three days in the grave	Matt. 28:1–15 Mark 16:1–8 Luke 24:1–7 John 20:1–10
Apostles	Freed from prison by an angel	Acts 5:17–20
Dorcas	Raised from the dead by Peter	Acts 9:36–41
Peter	Released from prison by an angel	Acts 12:1–11
Eutychus	Revived by Paul after his fall from a window	Acts 20:1–12
Paul	Delivered from a pressing burden (unnamed) in Asia	2 Cor. 1:8–11
Paul	Delivered unharmed to the island of Malta after a shipwreck	Acts 28:1

Philip's Travels

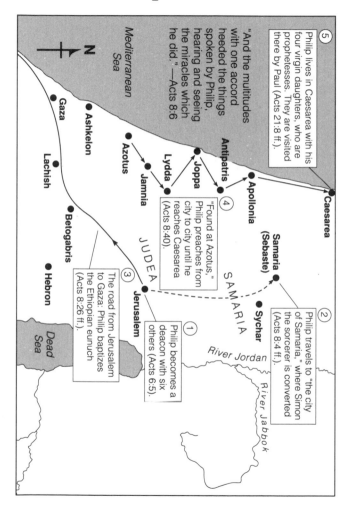

① Philip becomes a deacon with six others (Acts 6:5).

② Philip travels to "the city of Samaria," where Simon the sorcerer is converted (Acts 8:4 ff.).

③ The road from Jerusalem to Gaza: Philip baptizes the Ethiopian eunuch (Acts 8:26 ff.).

④ "Found at Azotus," Philip preaches from city to city until he reaches Caesarea (Acts 8:40).

⑤ Philip lives in Caesarea with his four virgin daughters, who are prophetesses. They are visited there by Paul (Acts 21:8 ff.).

"And the multitudes with one accord heeded the things spoken by Philip, hearing and seeing the miracles which he did." —Acts 8:6

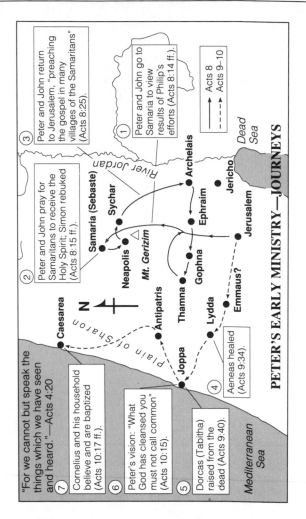

PETER'S EARLY MINISTRY—JOURNEYS

① Peter and John go to Samaria to view results of Philip's efforts (Acts 8:14 ff.).

→ Acts 8
- - → Acts 9–10

③ Peter and John return to Jerusalem, "preaching the gospel in many villages of the Samaritans" (Acts 8:25).

② Peter and John pray for Samaritans to receive the Holy Spirit; Simon rebuked (Acts 8:15 ff.).

⑦ "For we cannot but speak the things which we have seen and heard." —Acts 4:20

⑥ Cornelius and his household believe and are baptized (Acts 10:17 ff.).

⑥ Peter's vision: "What God has cleansed you must not call common" (Acts 10:15).

⑤ Dorcas (Tabitha) raised from the dead (Acts 9:40).

④ Aeneas healed (Acts 9:34).

Dead Sea

River Jordan

Archelais

Ephraim

Jericho

Jerusalem

Samaria (Sebaste)

Sychar

Neapolis

Mt. Gerizim

Gophna

Thamna

Emmaus?

Antipatris

Joppa

Lydda

Caesarea

Plain of Sharon

Mediterranean Sea

N

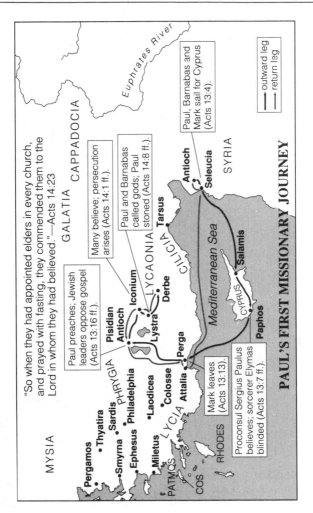

"So when they had appointed elders in every church, and prayed with fasting, they commended them to the Lord in whom they had believed." —Acts 14:23

Paul, Barnabas and Mark sail for Cyprus (Acts 13:4).

Many believe; persecution arises (Acts 14:1 ff.).

Paul and Barnabas called gods; Paul stoned (Acts 14:8 ff.).

Paul preaches; Jewish leaders oppose gospel (Acts 13:16 ff.).

Mark leaves (Acts 13:13).

Proconsul Sergius Paulus believes; sorcerer Elymas blinded (Acts 13:7 ff.).

→ outward leg
→ return leg

PAUL'S FIRST MISSIONARY JOURNEY

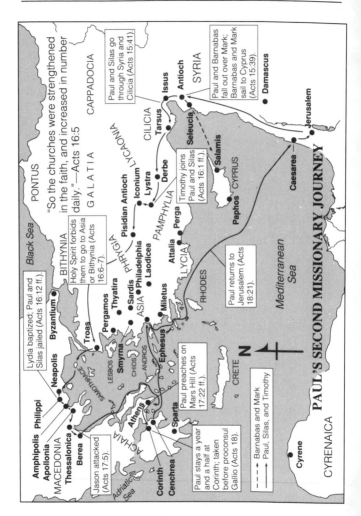

PAUL'S SECOND MISSIONARY JOURNEY

Paul and Silas go through Syria and Cilicia (Acts 15:41).

Paul and Barnabas fall out over Mark; Barnabas and Mark sail to Cyprus (Acts 15:39).

"So the churches were strengthened in the faith, and increased in number daily."—Acts 16:5

Holy Spirit forbids them to go to Asia or Bithynia (Acts 16:6-7).

Timothy joins Paul and Silas (Acts 16:1 ff.).

Paul returns to Jerusalem (Acts 18:21).

Lydia baptized; Paul and Silas jailed (Acts 16:12 ff.).

Paul preaches on Mars Hill (Acts 17:22 ff.).

Jason attacked (Acts 17:5).

Paul stays a year and a half at Corinth; taken before proconsul Gallio (Acts 18).

- - - → Barnabas and Mark
——→ Paul, Silas, and Timothy

CAPPADOCIA
PONTUS
SYRIA
Issus
Antioch
Damascus
Jerusalem
CILICIA
Tarsus
Seleucia
Salamis
CYPRUS
Paphos
Caesarea
GALATIA
LYCAONIA
PHRYGIA
Pisidian Antioch
Iconium
Lystra
Derbe
PAMPHYLIA
Perga
Attalia
LYCIA
BITHYNIA
Black Sea
Byzantium
Troas
Pergamos
Thyatira
Sardis
Philadelphia
Laodicea
ASIA
Smyrna
Ephesus
Miletus
LESBOS
CHIOS
ANDROS
RHODES
CRETE
Mediterranean Sea
Neapolis
Philippi
Amphipolis
Apollonia
Thessalonica
Berea
MACEDONIA
SAMOTHRACE
Athens
Sparta
ACHAIA
Corinth
Cenchrea
Adriatic Sea
CYRENAICA
Cyrene
N

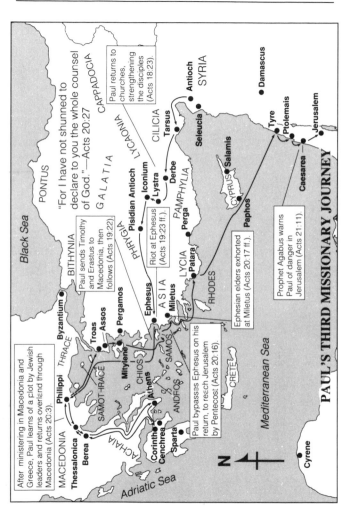

After ministering in Macedonia and Greece, Paul learns of a plot by Jewish leaders and returns overland through Macedonia (Acts 20:3).

"For I have not shunned to declare to you the whole counsel of God." —Acts 20:27

Paul returns to churches, strengthening the disciples (Acts 18:23).

Paul sends Timothy and Erastus to Macedonia, then follows (Acts 19:22).

Riot at Ephesus (Acts 19:23 ff.).

Paul bypasses Ephesus on his return, to reach Jerusalem by Pentecost (Acts 20:16).

Ephesian elders exhorted at Miletus (Acts 20:17 ff.).

Prophet Agabus warns Paul of danger in Jerusalem (Acts 21:11).

PAUL'S THIRD MISSIONARY JOURNEY

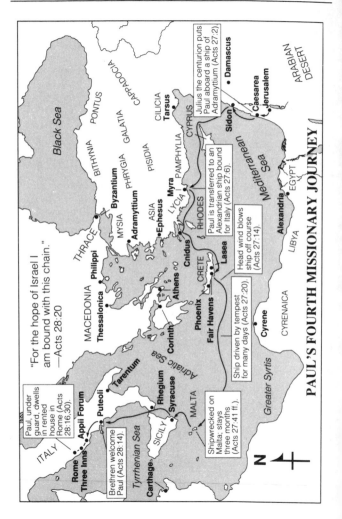

PAUL'S FOURTH MISSIONARY JOURNEY

Julius the centurion puts Paul aboard a ship of Adramyttium (Acts 27:2).

Paul is transferred to an Alexandrian ship bound for Italy (Acts 27:6).

Head wind blows ship off course (Acts 27:14).

Ship driven by tempest for many days (Acts 27:20).

"For the hope of Israel I am bound with this chain." —Acts 28:20

Paul, under guard, dwells in rented house in Rome (Acts 28:16,30).

Brethren welcome Paul (Acts 28:14).

Shipwrecked on Malta; stays three months (Acts 27:41 ff.).

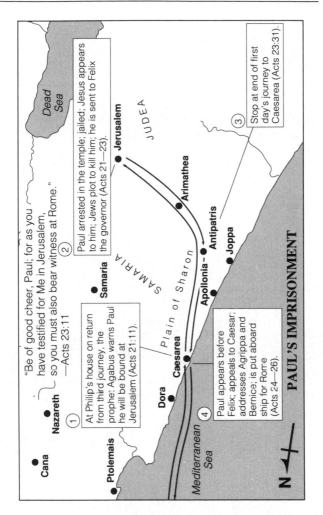

"Be of good cheer, Paul; for as you have testified for Me in Jerusalem, so you must also bear witness at Rome." —Acts 23:11

② Paul arrested in the temple; jailed; Jesus appears to him; Jews plot to kill him; he is sent to Felix the governor (Acts 21—23).

③ Stop at end of first day's journey to Caesarea (Acts 23:31).

① At Philip's house on return from third journey, the prophet Agabus warns Paul he will be bound at Jerusalem (Acts 21:11).

④ Paul appears before Felix; appeals to Caesar; addresses Agrippa and Bernice; is put aboard ship for Rome (Acts 24—26).

PAUL'S IMPRISONMENT

Dead Sea

Jerusalem

JUDEA

Arimathea

Antipatris

Joppa

Apollonia

Samaria

SAMARIA

Plain of Sharon

Caesarea

Dora

Nazareth

Cana

Ptolemais

Mediterranean Sea

N

Visions

In New Testament times, God often used visions to make His will known, particularly with church leaders.

Personality	Message of Vision	Reference
Paul	Converted to Christianity in a blinding vision of Christ on the Damascus road	Acts 9:3–9
Ananias	Instructed to minister to Saul in Damascus	Acts 9:10–16
Cornelius	Instructed to ask Peter to come to Joppa	Acts 10:3–6
Peter	Told to eat unclean animals—a message to accept the Gentiles	Acts 10:9–18, 28
Paul	Beckoned to do missionary work in the province of Macedonia	Acts 16:9
Paul	Assured of God's presence in Corinth	Acts 18:9, 10
Paul	Promised God's presence during his trip to Rome	Acts 23:11
Paul	Viewed the glories of the third heaven	2 Cor. 12:1–4
John	Received series of visions of future	Rev. 4:1—22:11

EIGHT

THE EPISTLES OF PAUL

◆

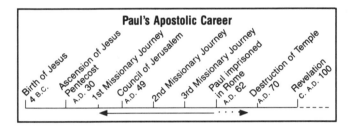

Paul's Apostolic Career

Birth of Jesus 4 B.C. | Ascension of Jesus Pentecost A.D. 30 | 1st Missionary Journey | Council of Jerusalem A.D. 49 | 2nd Missionary Journey | 3rd Missionary Journey | Paul imprisoned in Rome A.D. 62 | Destruction of Temple A.D. 70 | Revelation C. A.D. 100

The Career of the Apostle Paul

Origin: Tarsus in Cilicia (Acts 22:3); tribe of Benjamin (Phil. 3:5)

Training: Learned tentmaking (Acts 18:3); studied under Gamaliel (Acts 22:3)

Early Religion: Hebrew and Pharisee (Phil. 3:5); persecuted Christians (Acts 8:1–3)

Salvation: Met the risen Christ on the road to Damascus (Acts 9:1–8); received the infilling of the Holy Spirit on the street called Straight (Acts 9:17)

Called to Missions: Church at Antioch was instructed by the Holy Spirit to send out Paul to the work (Acts 13:1–3); carried the gospel to the Gentiles (Gal. 2:7–10)

Survey of Paul's Epistles

Book	No. of Chapters	Theme	Place Written	Date Written	Recipients
Romans	16	The Righteousness of God	Corinth	Winter 57	Beloved of God in Rome, called to be saints (1:1)
1 Corinthians	16	Solving Divisions and Disorders	Ephesus	56–57	Church of God at Corinth, those sanctified in Christ Jesus (1:2)
2 Corinthians	13	The Ministry of Reconciliation	Macedonia	56–57	Church of God at Corinth with all the saints in Achaia (1:1)
Galatians	6	Freedom in Christ	Antioch(?)	48–49 or 55–57	Churches of Galatia (1:2)
Ephesians	6	The Church: The Body of Christ	Rome	60–63	Saints of Ephesus, faithful in Christ Jesus (1:1)
Philippians	4	Joyful Christian Living	Rome	60–63	Saints in Christ Jesus in Philippi with the bishops and deacons (1:1)

Colossians	4	The Cosmic Christ	Rome	60–63	Saints and faithful brethren in Christ at Colosse (1:2)
1 Thessalonians	5	The Coming of Christ	Corinth	51–52	Church of the Thessalonians in God the Father and the Lord Jesus Christ (1:1)
2 Thessalonians	3	The Day of the Lord	Corinth	51–52	Church of the Thessalonians in God our Father and the Lord Jesus Christ (1:1)
1 Timothy	6	Pastoral Advice	Macedonia (?)	62–66	Timothy, a true son in the faith (1:2)
2 Timothy	4	A Farewell Word of Encouragement	Rome	66–67	Timothy, a beloved son (1:2)
Titus	3	A Christian Conduct Manual	Macedonia(?)	63–66	Titus, a true son in our common faith (1:4)
Philemon	1	Receiving a Slave as a Brother	Rome	60–63	Philemon, our beloved friend and fellow laborer (1:1)

Timeline of Paul's Epistles
(Dates are probable, not certain)

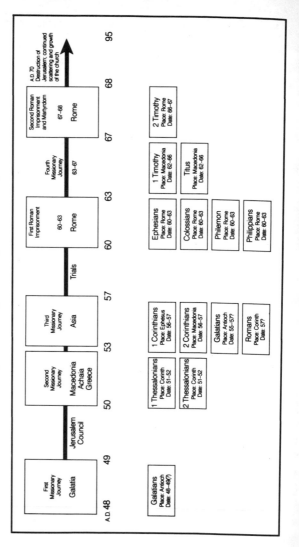

Roles:	Spoke up for the church at Antioch at the council of Jerusalem (Acts 15:1–35); opposed Peter (Gal. 2:11–21); disputed with Barnabas about John Mark (Acts 15:36–41)
Achievements:	Three extended missionary journeys (Acts 13—20); founded numerous churches in Asia Minor, Greece and possibly Spain (Rom. 15:24, 28); wrote letters to numerous churches and various individuals which now make up one-fourth of our New Testament
End of Life:	Following arrest in Jerusalem, was sent to Rome (Acts 21:27; 28:16–31); according to Christian tradition, released from prison allowing further missionary work in Macedonia; rearrested, imprisoned again in Rome, and beheaded outside of the city

Paul's Epistle to the ROMANS

◆

LANDMARKS OF ROMANS

Key Word: *The Righteousness of God*

The theme of Romans is found in 1:16, 17: God offers the gift of His righteousness to everyone who comes to Christ by faith.

Overview of Romans

FOCUS	Revelation of God's Righteousness			Vindication of God's Righteousness			Application of God's Righteousness	
REFERENCE	1:1 ———	3:1 ———	6:1 ———	9:1 ———	9:30 ———	11:1 ———	12:1 ———	14:1 —16:27
DIVISION	Need for God's Righteousness	Imputation of God's Righteousness	Demonstration of God's Righteousness	Israel's Past: Election	Israel's Present: Rejection	Israel's Future: Restoration	Christian Duties	Christian Liberties
TOPIC	Sin	Salvation	Sanctification	Sovereignty			Service	
	Doctrinal						Behavioral	
LOCATION	Probably Written in Corinth							
TIME	c. A.D. 56–57							

Key Verses: *Romans 1:16, 17 and 3:21–25*
Key Chapters: *Romans 6–8*

Foundational to all teaching on the spiritual life is the central passage of Romans 6—8. The answers to the questions of how to be delivered from sin, how to live a balanced life under grace, and how to live the victorious Christian life through the power of the Holy Spirit are all contained here.

The Christian Life

Although the theological depth of Paul's epistle to the Romans is profound, the apostle does not neglect the practical aspects of the Christian life. Given what God has done for us and in us through Jesus Christ, Paul exhorts each believer to honor God with a life of sacrificial obedience that is "holy, acceptable to God" as the chart below explains.

Description of the Christian	Result
Presents himself to God (12:1)	Becomes a sacrifice that is living, holy, and pleasing to God (12:1)
Receives transformation by a renewed mind (12:2)	Discovers and displays the will of God (12:2)
Has spiritual gifts according to grace from God (12:6–8)	Uses spiritual gifts as part of Christ's body (12:6)
Honors civil law (13:1)	Honors God (13:1)
Loves others (13:8)	Fulfills God's law (13:8)
Pursues peace (14:19)	Serves to edify all (14:19)
Becomes like-minded toward others (15:5)	Glorifies God with others (15:6)

The City of Rome

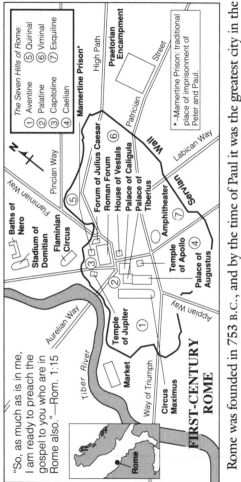

FIRST-CENTURY ROME

The Seven Hills of Rome:
① Aventine ⑤ Quirinal
② Palatine ⑥ Viminal
③ Capitoline ⑦ Esquiline
④ Caelian

*—Mamertine Prison: traditional place of imprisonment of Peter and Paul.

"So, as much as is in me, I am ready to preach the gospel to you who are in Rome also."—Rom. 1:15

Rome was founded in 753 B.C., and by the time of Paul it was the greatest city in the world with over one million inhabitants. It was full of magnificent buildings, but the majority of people were slaves; opulence and squalor coexisted in this imperial city.

The church in Rome was well known (1:8), and it had been established for several years by the time of this letter. The believers there were numerous, and evidently they met in several places (16:1–16). The Roman historian Tacitus referred to the Christians who were persecuted under Nero in A.D. 64 as "an immense multitude."

Paul's First Epistle to the
CORINTHIANS

◆

LANDMARKS OF FIRST CORINTHIANS

Key Word: *Correction of Carnal Living*

The cross of Christ is a message that is designed to transform the lives of believers and make them different as people and as a corporate body from the surrounding world. However, the Corinthians are destroying their Christian testimony because of immorality and disunity.

Key Verses: *First Corinthians 6:19, 20 and 10:12, 13*

Key Chapter: *First Corinthians 13*

This chapter has won the hearts of people across the world as the best definition of "love" ever penned.

◆

The Way of Love
(1 Corinthians 13)

Paul valued the gift of prophecy highly, and the Corinthians placed a premium on spectacular gifts such as speaking in tongues, as well as on the gifts of understanding spiritual mysteries and faith to do dramatic miracles. Yet even these spiritual gifts do no good in God's sight unless we live in love.

continued on page 263

Overview of First Corinthians

FOCUS	Answer to Chloe's Report of Divisions		Answer to Report of Fornication			Answer to Letter of Questions				
REFERENCE	1:1 ——— 1:18 ———		5:1 ——— 6:1 ———		6:12 ——— 7:1 ———		8:1 ——— 11:2 ———		15:1 — 16:1—16:24	
DIVISION	Report of Divisions	Reason for Divisions	Incest	Litigation	Immorality	Marriage	Offerings to Idols	Public Worship	Resurrection	Collection for Jerusalem
TOPIC	Divisions in the Church		Disorder in the Church				Difficulties in the Church			
	Concern		Condemnation				Counsel			
LOCATION	Written in Ephesus									
TIME	c. A.D. 56									

The Agora of Corinth

Corinth was a very sophisticated cosmopolitan city, as this map indicates.

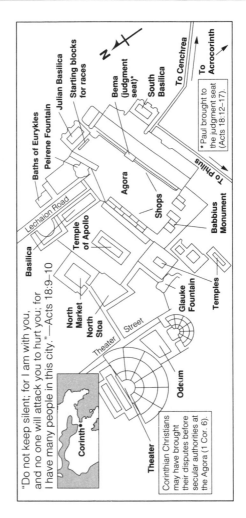

"Do not keep silent; for I am with you, and no one will attack you to hurt you; for I have many people in this city."—Acts 18:9–10

Corinthian Christians may have brought their disputes before secular authorities at the Agora (1 Cor. 6).

* Paul brought to the judgment seat (Acts 18:12–17).

Map labels: To Acrocorinth; To Cenchrea; To Philius; N; Starting blocks for races; Julian Basilica; Bema (judgment seat)*; South Basilica; Baths of Eurykles; Peirene Fountain; Agora; Shops; Babbius Monument; Lechaion Road; Basilica; Temple of Apollo; North Market; North Stoa; Glauke Fountain; Temples; Street; Theater; Odeum; Theater

Corinth

New Testament Lists of Spiritual Gifts

The New Testament provides us with several lists of spiritual gifts. No one list is exhaustive, and the contents of each list depend on the specific purpose of the author. In Romans 12, Paul deals with gifts in general terms, while in 1 Corinthians 12 Paul stresses the gifts which build up the church as a whole rather than the more spectacular gifts, such as tongues, which may confer individual benefit but were subject to abuse by the Corinthian Christians.

Romans 12:6–8	1 Cor. 12:8–10	1 Cor. 12:28–30	Eph. 4:11	1 Peter 4:9–11
Prophecy	Word of Wisdom	Apostleship	Apostleship	Speaking
Serving	Word of Knowledge	Prophecy	Prophecy	Serving
Teaching	Faith	Teaching	Evangelism	
Exhortation	Healings	Miracles	Pastor/Teacher	
Giving	Miracles	Healing		
Leading	Prophecy	Helping		
Showing Mercy	Discerning of Spirits	Administrating		
	Tongues	Tongues		
	Interpretation of Tongues	Interpretation of Tongues		

Love is . . .	Without Love . . .	Love is Greater Than . . .
Patient, kind, unselfish, truthful, hopeful, enduring (vv. 4–7)	Tongues are mere noise (v. 1)	Prophecies, which will fail (v. 8)
Not envious, proud, self-centered, rude, or provoked to anger (vv. 4, 5)	Prophecy, mysteries, knowledge, and faith amount to nothing (v. 2)	Tongues, which will cease (v. 8)
	Good deeds are unprofitable (v. 3)	Knowledge, which will vanish (v. 8)

Love is one of the dynamic terms Paul uses to speak of the holy life enabled by the fullness of the Holy Spirit. It encompasses motive and deed. Love is characteristic of the mature believer.

Paul's Second Epistle to the CORINTHIANS

—————◆—————

LANDMARKS OF SECOND CORINTHIANS

Key Word: *Paul's Defense of His Ministry*

The major theme of 2 Corinthians is Paul's defense of his apostolic credentials and authority.

Key Verses: *Second Corinthians 4:5, 6 and 5:17–19*

Overview of Second Corinthians

FOCUS	Explanation of Paul's Ministry			Collection for the Saints		Vindication of Paul's Apostleship		
REFERENCE	1:1 ——— 2:14 ———	6:11 ———	8:1 ———	8:7 ———	10:1 ———	11:1 ———	12:14 ——— 13:14	
DIVISION	His Change of Plans	Philosophy of Ministry	Exhortations to the Corinthians	Example of the Macedonians	Exhortation to the Corinthians	Answers His Accusers	Defends His Apostleship	Announces His Upcoming Visit
TOPIC	Character of Paul			Collection for Saints		Credentials of Paul		
	Ephesus to Macedonia: Change of Itinerary			Macedonia: Preparation for Visit		To Corinth: Imminent Visit		
LOCATION	Written in Macedonia							
TIME	c. A.D. 56							

Key Chapters: *Second Corinthians 8 and 9*

These chapters are one unit and comprise the most complete revelation of God's plan for giving found anywhere in the Scriptures.

Paul's Epistle to the
GALATIANS

LANDMARKS OF GALATIANS

Key Word: *Freedom from the Law*

This epistle shows that the believer is no longer under the law but is saved by faith alone. Galatians is the Christian's Declaration of Independence.

Key Verses: *Galatians 2:20, 21 and 5:1*

Key Chapter: *Galatians 5*

The impact of the truth concerning freedom is staggering: freedom must not be used "as an opportunity for the flesh, but through love serve one another" (5:13). This chapter records the power, "Walk in the Spirit" (5:16), and the results, "the fruit of the Spirit" (5:22), of that freedom.

Overview of Galatians

FOCUS	Gospel of Grace Defended		Gospel of Grace Explained		Gospel of Grace Applied	
REFERENCE	1:1 ——— 2:1 ———		3:1 ——— 4:1 ———		5:1 ——— 6:1 ——— 6:18	
DIVISION	Paul's Apostleship	Paul's Authority	Bondage of Law	Freedom of Grace	Fruit of the Spirit	Fruits of the Spirit
TOPIC	Biographical Explanation		Doctrinal Exposition		Practical Exhortation	
	Authentication of Liberty		Argumentation for Liberty		Application of Liberty	
LOCATION	South Galatian Theory: Syrian Antioch North Galatian Theory: Ephesus or Macedonia					
TIME	South Galatian Theory: A.D. 48 North Galatian Theory: A.D. 53–56					

The Region of Galatia

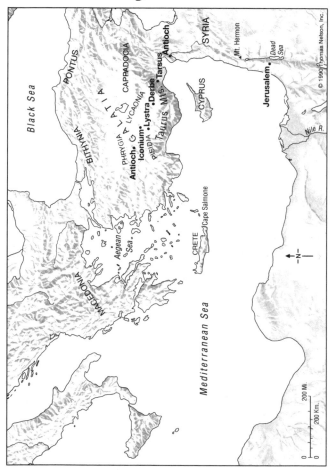

Overview of Ephesians

FOCUS	The Position of the Christian			The Practice of the Christian			
REFERENCE	1:1 ——— 1:15 ———	2:1 ———	3:14 ———	4:1 ———	4:17 ———	5:22 ———	6:10 ——— 6:24
DIVISION	Praise for Redemption	Prayer for Revelation	Position of the Christian	Prayer for Realization	Unity in the Church	Holiness in Life	Responsibilities at Home and Work	Conduct in the Conflict
TOPIC	Belief				Behavior			
	Privileges of the Christian				Responsibilites of the Christian			
LOCATION	Rome							
TIME	A.D. 60–61							

Law and Grace
(Galatians 3—4)

The Function		The Effect	
Of Law	*Of Grace*	*Of Law*	*Of Grace*
Based on works (3:10)	Based on faith (3:11, 12)	Works put us under a curse (3:10)	Justifies us by faith (3:3, 24)
Our guardian (3:23; 4:2)	Centered in Christ (3:24)	Keeps us for faith (3:23)	Christ lives in us (2:20)
Our tutor (3:24)	Our certificate of freedom (4:30, 31)	Brings us to Christ (3:24)	Adopts us as sons and heirs (4:7)

The law functions to (1) declare our guilt, (2) drive us to Christ, and (3) direct us in a life of obedience. However, the law is powerless to save.

Paul's Epistle to the EPHESIANS

◆

LANDMARKS OF EPHESIANS

Key Word: *Building the Body of Christ*

Ephesians focuses on the believer's responsibility to walk in accordance with his heavenly calling in Christ Jesus and encouraging the body of Christ to maturity in Him.

Key Verses: *Ephesians 2:8-10 and 4:1-3*

Key Chapter: *Ephesians 6*

Even though the Christian is blessed "with every spiritual blessing in the heavenly places in Christ" (1:3), spiritual warfare is still the daily experience of the Christian while in the world.

◆

Blessings in Christ
(Ephesians 1)

Grace refers to the beneficial actions of God in which He reveals Himself, His gifts, and His life—all bestowals which grow out of His love rather than any sinful person's worth or merit. Furthermore, the salvation of the believer is ensured by the work of all three Persons of the Trinity—the loving choice of the Father, the redeeming work of the Son, and the sealing of the Holy Spirit.

Benefit:	Christ's spiritual blessings in heaven (v. 3); the forgiveness of sins (v. 7)
Origin:	Divine choice from eternity past (v. 4); the good pleasure of God's will (v. 5)
Purpose:	Love manifested in holiness and blamelessness (v. 4); to be joined with Christ (v. 10)
Privilege:	Adoption into God's family as beneficiaries of Christ (v. 5)
Cost:	The blood of Christ (v. 7)
Means:	Having heard the truth, trusting in Christ (vv. 12, 13)
Assurance:	The Holy Spirit as the down payment of our inheritance (vv. 13, 14)

The Work of the Father: Election (1:3–6)
The Work of the Son: Redemption (1:7–12)
The Work of the Spirit: Protection (1:13, 14)

IN CHRIST I AM:
Blessed (v. 3)
Chosen (v. 4)
Predestined (v. 5)
Adopted (v. 5)
Accepted (v. 6)
Redeemed (v. 7)
Forgiven (v. 7)
Enlightened (vv. 8, 9)
Given an Inheritance (v. 11)
Sealed (v. 13)
Assured (v. 14)

Salvation: Our Greatest Possession

The first three chapters of Ephesians list all the possessions of the Christian and detail the riches of redemption.

Justification (Past Tense)	Sanctification (Present Tense)	Glorification (Future Tense)
Saved *immediately* fron sin's penalty	Saved *progressively* from sin's power	Saved *ultimately* from sin's presence

"For by grace you have been saved through
faith, and that not of yourselves;
it is the gift of God."
(Ephesians 2:8)

The City of Ephesus

Paul visited Ephesus at the end of his second missionary journey, where he left Priscilla and Aquila (Acts 18:18–21). Returning to the city on his third missionary journey, Paul spent nearly three years there (Acts 18:23–19:41).

"But now in Christ Jesus you who once were far off have been brought near by the blood of Christ." —Eph. 2:13

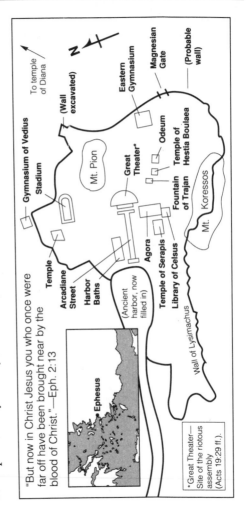

*Great Theater— Site of the riotous assembly (Acts 19:29 ff.).

Labels on map: N; To temple of Diana; Magnesian Gate; (Probable wall); (Wall excavated); Eastern Gymnasium; Gymnasium of Vedius; Stadium; Mt. Pion; Great Theater*; Odeum; Temple of Hestia Boulaea; Fountain of Trajan; Mt. Koressos; Agora; Temple of Serapis; Library of Celsus; Temple; Arcadiane Street; Harbor Baths; (Ancient harbor, now filled in); Wall of Lysimachus; Ephesus

Paul's Epistle to the
PHILIPPIANS

---◆---

LANDMARKS OF PHILIPPIANS

Key Word: *To Live Is Christ*

Central to Philippians is the concept of "For to me, to live *is* Christ, and to die *is* gain" (1:21).

Key Verses: *Philippians 1:21 and 4:12*

Key Chapter: *Philippians 2*

The grandeur of the truth of the New Testament seldom exceeds the revelation of the humility of Jesus Christ when He left heaven to become a servant of man.

---◆---

The Mind of Christ
(Genesis 1–3; Philippians 2)

Philippians 2 contrasts vividly the mind of Christ, the second Adam, with that of the first Adam.

Adam	Christ
Made in the divine image.	Is the form and very essence of God.
Thought it a prize to be grasped at to be as God.	Thought it not a prize to be grasped at to be as God.
Aspired to a reputation.	Made Himself of no reputation.

Overview of Philippians

FOCUS	Account of Circumstances	The Mind of Christ	The Knowledge of Christ	The Peace of Christ
REFERENCE	1:1 ———	2:1 ———	3:1 ———	4:1 ——— 4:23
DIVISION	Partake of Christ	People of Christ	Pursuit of Christ	Power of Christ
TOPIC	Suffering	Submission	Salvation	Sanctification
	Experience	Examples	Exhortation	
LOCATION	Rome			
TIME	c. A.D. 60			

Adam	Christ
Spurned the role of God's servant.	Took upon Himself the form of a bondservant (slave).
Seeking to be like God.	Coming in the likeness of men.
And being made a man (of dust, now doomed),	And being found in appearance as a man,
He exalted himself,	He humbled Himself,
And became disobedient unto death.	And became obedient to the point of death.
He was condemned and disgraced.	God highly exalted Him and gave Him the name and position of Lord.

Seeking Christ
(Philippians)

The Book of Philippians teaches that the Christian life focuses on seeking Christ and the pursuit of intimacy with God. This pursuit consists of devoting oneself to knowing Jesus Christ, and one measure of spiritual maturity is the degree to which this pursuit becomes our consuming focus and desire.

SEEK
- Christ above all (1:21; 3:7, 8) and FIND righteousness in Christ and the power of His resurrection (3:9–11)
- Christlike humility (2:5–7) and FIND God's will in the believer (2:12, 13)
- A divinely appointed goal (3:14) and FIND the prize of eternal salvation (3:14)
- All things that are true, noble, just, pure, lovely, virtuous, and praiseworthy (4:8) and FIND the presence of the God of peace (4:9)

Overview of Colossians

FOCUS	Supremacy of Christ			Submission to Christ		
REFERENCE	1:1 ——— 1:15 ———		2:4 ——— 3:1 ———		3:5 ——— 4:7 ———	4:18
DIVISION	Introduction	Preeminence of Christ	Freedom in Christ	Position of the Believer	Practice of the Believer	Conclusion
TOPIC	What Christ Did for Us			What Christ Does Through Us		
	Doctrinal			Practical		
LOCATION	Rome					
TIME	A.D. 60–61					

Paul's Epistle to the COLOSSIANS

◆

LANDMARKS OF COLOSSIANS

Key Word: *The Preeminence of Christ*

The resounding theme in Colossians is the preeminence and sufficiency of Christ in all things. The believer is complete in Him alone and lacks nothing because "in Him dwells all the fullness of the Godhead bodily" (2:9).

Key Verses: *Colossians 2:9, 10 and 3:1, 2*

Key Chapter: *Colossians 3*

Chapter 3 links the three themes of Colossians together showing their cause and effect relationship: Because the believer is risen with Christ (3:1–4), he is to put off the old man and put on the new (3:5–17), which will result in holiness in all relationships (3:18–25).

◆

Hymns and Songs of the New Testament

As is evident in the Old Testament, the Hebrew faith emphasized the joy of singing to the Lord, but Christianity is even more profoundly a singing faith. Singing can help to make teaching and preaching even more useful. The Colossians were to emphasize the ministry of teach-

continued on page 280

The Preeminence of Christ
(Colossians)

In addition to these descriptions of Christ in Colossians, three other New Testament books feature similarly exalted description—John 1:1–14; Philippians 2; and Hebrews 1 and 2.

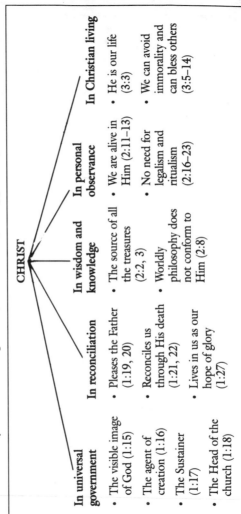

CHRIST

In universal government
- The visible image of God (1:15)
- The agent of creation (1:16)
- The Sustainer (1:17)
- The Head of the church (1:18)

In reconciliation
- Pleases the Father (1:19, 20)
- Reconciles us through His death (1:21, 22)
- Lives in us as our hope of glory (1:27)

In wisdom and knowledge
- The source of all the treasures (2:2, 3)
- Worldly philosophy does not conform to Him (2:8)

In personal observance
- We are alive in Him (2:11–13)
- No need for legalism and ritualism (2:16–23)

In Christian living
- He is our life (3:3)
- We can avoid immorality and can bless others (3:5–14)

Hymns and Songs of the New Testament

Personality	Description	Biblical Reference
Jesus and Disciples	A song in the Upper Room as they celebrated the Passover together just before the arrest of Jesus	Matt. 26:30
Mary	The Song of Mary, upon learning that she as a virgin would give birth to Jesus	Luke 1:46–55
Zacharias	A song of joy at the circumcision of his son, who would serve as the Messiah's forerunner	Luke 1:68–79
Paul and Silas	A song of praise to God at midnight from their prison cell in Philippi	Acts 16:25
All Believers	The spiritual songs of thanksgiving and joy, which God wants all believers to sing	Eph. 5:19 Col 3:16
144,000 Believers	A new song of the redeemed in heaven, sung to glorify God	Rev. 14:1–3

ing and admonition by the singing of psalms, hymns, and spiritual songs (see chart p. 279).

Many elements of Ephesians parallel those of Colossians, including the songs of thanksgiving. The chart below includes some of those parallels.

A Comparison of Ephesians and Colossians

Ephesians	Colossians
Jesus Christ: Lord of the *church*	Jesus Christ: Lord of the *cosmos*
Emphasis on the *church* as the body of Christ but also affirms Christ as Head of the church.	Emphasis on *Christ* as the Head of the cosmos and the church.
Less personal and probably a *circular* epistle.	More personal and *local*-church-oriented.
Address the errors of false teaching less directly (heresy is not yet a major danger).	Speaks to the errors of false doctrine directly (heresy is more threatening).
Common themes treated extensively.	Common themes treated briefly.

Paul's First Epistle to the THESSALONIANS

◆

LANDMARKS OF FIRST THESSALONIANS

Key Words: *Holiness in Light of Christ's Return*

Throughout this letter is an unmistakable emphasis upon steadfastness in the Lord and a continuing growth in faith and love in view of the return of Christ.

Key Verses: *First Thessalonians 3:12, 13 and 4:16–18*

Key Chapter: *First Thessalonians 4*

Chapter 4 includes the central passage of the epistles on the coming of the Lord when the dead in Christ shall rise first, and those who remain are caught up together with them in the clouds.

◆

A Comparison of Emphases in 1 and 2 Thessalonians

Second Thessalonians is the theological sequel to First Thessalonians. Not long after receiving 1 Thessalonians from Paul, some of the Thessalonian believers fell prey to false teaching, thinking the final day of the Lord had already begun. Paul wrote this brief letter to correct that error by pointing out that certain identifiable events will precede the final day of the Lord, and to encourage the

Overview of First Thessalonians

FOCUS	Reflections on the Thessalonians			Instructions to the Thessalonians			
REFERENCE	1:1 ———	2:1 ———	2:17 ———	4:1 ———	4:13 ———	5:1 ———	5:12 ——— 5:28
DIVISION	Commendation for Growth	Founding of the Church	Strengthening of the Church	Direction for Growth	The Dead in Christ	The Day of the Lord	Holy Living
TOPIC	Personal Experience			Practical Exhortation			
	Looking Back			Looking Forward			
LOCATION	Written in Corinth						
TIME	c. A.D. 51						

Thessalonian believers, whose faith was being tested by persecution. The chart below notes other distinctions between the two letters.

1 Thessalonians	2 Thessalonians
Addresses how the Thessalonians were evangelized as they received the Word of God	Addresses how the Thessalonians are being edified, noting their progress in faith, love, and patience
The imminency and importance of the Lord's return is emphasized	Misunderstandings about the Lord's return are corrected
The saints are comforted and encouraged	The saints are assured of God's judgment on His enemies

Paul's Second Epistle to the THESSALONIANS

❖

LANDMARKS OF SECOND THESSALONIANS

Key Word: *Understanding the Day of the Lord*

The theme of this epistle is an understanding of the day of the Lord and the resulting lifestyle changes.

Key Verses: *Second Thessalonians 2:2, 3 and 3:5, 6*

Key Chapter: *Second Thessalonians 2*

The second chapter is written to correct the fallacious teaching that the day of the Lord has already come upon the Thessalonian church.

❖

Overview of Second Thessalonians

FOCUS	Encouragement in Persecution		Explanation of the Day of the Lord		Exhortation to the Church	
REFERENCE	1:1 ——— 1:5 ———	1:11 ———	2:1 ———	2:13 ———	3:1 ———	3:6 ——— 3:18
DIVISION	Thanksgiving for Growth	Encouragement in Persecution	Prayer for Blessing	Events Preceding	Comfort of the Believer	Wait Patiently	Withdraw
TOPIC	Discouraged Believers		Disturbed Believers		Disobedient Believers	
	Thanksgiving for Their Life		Instruction of Their Doctrine		Correction of Their Behavior	
LOCATION	Written in Corinth					
TIME	c. A.D. 51					

Paul's First Epistle to
TIMOTHY

◆

LANDMARKS OF FIRST TIMOTHY

Key Word: *Leadership Manual*

The theme of this epistle is Timothy's organization and oversight of the Asian churches as a faithful minister of God. Paul writes so that Timothy will have effective guidelines for his work during Paul's absence in Macedonia (3:14, 15).

Key Verses: *First Timothy 3:15, 16 and 6:11, 12*

Key Chapter: *First Timothy 3*

Listed in chapter 3 are the qualifications for the leaders of God's church, the elders and deacons. Notably absent are qualities of worldly success or position. Instead, Paul enumerates character qualities demonstrating that true leadership emanates from our walk with God rather than from achievements or vocational success.

◆

Spiritual Leadership
(1 Timothy 3)

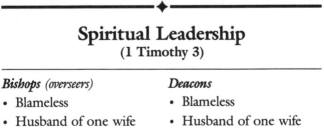

Bishops (overseers)	*Deacons*
• Blameless	• Blameless
• Husband of one wife	• Husband of one wife
• Temperate	• Reverent

Overview of First Timothy

FOCUS	Doctrine	Public Worship	False Teachers	Church Discipline	Pastoral Motives
REFERENCE	1:1 ———	2:1 ———	4:1 ———	5:1 ———	6:1 ——— 6:21
DIVISION	Problem of False Doctrine	Public Worship and Leadership	Preserve True Doctrine	Prescriptions for Widows and Elders	Pastoral Motivations
TOPIC	Warning	Worship	Wisdom	Widows	Wealth
	Dangers of False Doctrine	Directions for Worship	Defense Against False Teachers	Duties Toward Others	Dealings with Riches
LOCATION	Written in Macedonia				
TIME	c. A.D. 62–63				

Bishops (overseers)

- Sober-minded
- Of good behavior
- Hospitable
- Able to teach
- Not given to wine
- Not violent
- Not greedy for money
- Gentle
- Not quarrelsome
- Not covetous
- Rules his own house well
- Children in submission with all reverence
- Not a novice
- Good testimony with outsiders

Deacons

- Not double-tongued
- Not given to much wine
- Not greedy for money
- Holding the mystery of the faith with a pure conscience
- Tested
- Rules his own children and wife

Wives

- Reverent
- Not Slanderers
- Temperate
- Faithful in all things

Paul's Second Epistle to
TIMOTHY

◆

LANDMARKS OF SECOND TIMOTHY

Key Word: *Endurance in the Pastoral Ministry*

Paul commissions Timothy to endure faithfully and carry on the work that the condemned apostle must now

Overview of Second Timothy

FOCUS	Persevere in Present Testings			Endure in Future Testings		
REFERENCE	1:1 ——— 1:6 ———	2:1 ———	3:1 ———	4:1 ———	4:6 ——— 4:22	
DIVISION	Thanksgiving for Timothy's Faith	Reminder of Timothy's Responsibility	Characteristics of a Faithful Minister	Approaching Day of Apostasy	Charge to Preach the Word	Approaching Death of Paul
TOPIC	Power of the Gospel		Perseverance of the Gospel	Protector of the Gospel	Proclamation of the Gospel	
	Reminder		Requirements	Resistance	Requests	
LOCATION	Roman Prison					
TIME	c. A.D. 67					

relinquish, using the Word of God constantly in order to overcome growing obstacles to the spread of the gospel.

Key Verses: *Second Timothy 2:3, 4 and 3:14–17*

Key Chapter: *Second Timothy 2*

The second chapter of Second Timothy ought to be required daily reading for every pastor and full-time Christian worker. Paul lists the keys to an enduring ministry: a reproducing ministry (vv. 1, 2), an enduring successful ministry (vv. 3–13), a studying ministry (vv. 14–18), and a holy ministry (vv. 19–26).

———————————◆———————————

Timothy's Ministry
(2 Timothy)

In 2 Timothy, Paul writes as one who knows his days on earth are quickly drawing to a close. The chart on p. 290 gives details of this his second imprisonment. About to relinquish his heavy burdens, the godly apostle seeks to challenge and strengthen his faithful but somewhat timid associate, Timothy, in his difficult ministry in Ephesus. Despite his bleak circumstances, this is a letter of encouragement. Central to everything in 2 Timothy is the sure foundation of the Word of God.

Timothy must . . .	Because . . .
Share in suffering for the gospel (1:8; 2:3)	Through such sharing others will be saved (2:10)
Continue in sound doctrine (1:13; 2:15)	False doctrine spreads and leads to ungodliness (2:16, 17)

Timothy must . . .	Because . . .
Flee youthful lusts (2:22)	He must be cleansed and set apart for the Master's use (2:21)
Avoid contentiousness (2:23–25)	He must gently lead others to the truth (2:24–26)
Militantly preach the gospel (4:2)	Great apostasy is coming (4:3, 4)

A Comparison of Paul's Two Roman Imprisonments

First Imprisonment	Second Imprisonment
Acts 28—Wrote the Prison Epistles	2 Timothy
Accused by Jews of heresy and sedition	Persecuted by Rome and arrested as a criminal against the Empire
Local sporadic persecutions (A.D. 60–63)	Neronian persecution (A.D. 64–68)
Decent living conditions in a rented house (Acts 28:30, 31)	Poor conditions, in a cold, dark dungeon
Many friends visited him	Virtually alone (only Luke with him)
Many opportunities for Christian witness were available	Opportunities for witness were restricted
Was optimistic for release and freedom (Phil. 1:24–26)	Anticipated his execution (2 Tim. 4:6)

Paul's Epistle to
TITUS

---◆---

LANDMARKS OF TITUS

Key Word: *Conduct Manual for Church Living*

This brief letter focuses on Titus's role and responsibility in the organization and supervision of the churches in Crete. It is written to strengthen and exhort Titus to firmly exercise his authority as an apostolic representative to churches that need to be put in order.

Key Verses: *Titus 1:5 and 3:8*

Key Chapter: *Titus 2*

Summarized in Titus 2 are the key commands to be obeyed which insure godly relationships within the church.

---◆---

Overview of Titus

FOCUS	Appoint Elders		Set Things in Order	
REFERENCE	1:1 ——— 1:10	——— 2:1	——— 3:1	——— 3:15
DIVISION	Ordain Qualified Elders	Rebuke False Teachers	Speak Sound Doctrine	Maintain Good Works
TOPIC	Protection of Sound Doctrine		Practice of Sound Doctrine	
	Organization	Offenders	Operation	Obedience
LOCATION	Probably Written in Corinth			
TIME	c. A.D. 64			

Paul's Epistle to PHILEMON

♦

LANDMARKS OF PHILEMON

Key Word: *Forgiveness from Slavery*

Philemon develops the transition from bondage to brotherhood that is brought about by Christian love and forgiveness. Just as Philemon was shown mercy through the grace of Christ, so he must graciously forgive his repentant runaway who has returned as a brother in Christ.

Key Verses: *Philemon 16, 17*

♦

How Love Works
(Philemon)

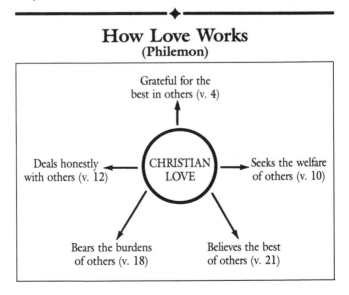

Grateful for the
best in others (v. 4)

Deals honestly
with others (v. 12)

CHRISTIAN
LOVE

Seeks the welfare
of others (v. 10)

Bears the burdens
of others (v. 18)

Believes the best
of others (v. 21)

Overview of Philemon

FOCUS	Prayer of Thanksgiving	Petition for Onesimus	Promise to Philemon
REFERENCE 1	——— 8 ———	——— 17 ———	——— 25
DIVISION	Commendation of Philemon's Life	Intercession for Onesimus	Confidence in Philemon's Obedience
TOPIC	Praise of Philemon	Plea of Paul	Pledge of Paul
	Character of Philemon	Conversion of Onesimus	Confidence of Paul
LOCATION		Rome	
TIME		c. A.D. 60–61	

NINE

THE GENERAL EPISTLES AND REVELATION

◆

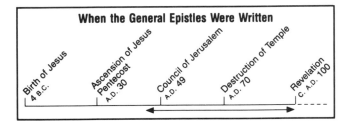

The Epistle to the HEBREWS

◆

LANDMARKS OF HEBREWS

Key Word: *The Superiority of Christ*

The basic theme of Hebrews is found in the word *better,* describing the superiority of Christ in His person and work (1:4; 6:9; 7:7, 19, 22; 8:6; 9:23; 10:34; 11:16, 35, 40; 12:24). The words *perfect* and *heavenly* are also prominent. He offers a better revelation, position, priesthood, covenant, sacrifice, and power.

Overview of Hebrews

FOCUS	Christ's Person			Christ's Work			The Walk of Faith		
REFERENCE	1:1 ——— 1:4 ——— 3:1 ——— 4:14 ——— 8:1 ——— 9:1 ——— 10:19 ——— 12:1 ——— 13:1 ——— 13:25								
DIVISION	Christ over Prophets	Christ over Angels	Christ over Moses	Priest-hood	Covenant	Sanctuary and Sacrifice	Assurance of Faith	Endurance of Faith	Exhortation to Love
TOPIC	Majesty of Christ			Ministry of Christ			Ministers for Christ		
	Doctrine						Discipline		
LOCATION	Place of Writing Unknown								
TIME	c. A.D. 64–68								

Key Verses: *Hebrews 4:14–16 and 12:1, 2*

Key Chapter: *Hebrews 11*

The hall of fame of the Scriptures is located in Hebrews 11 and records those who willingly took God at His word even when there was nothing to cling to but His promise.

───────────◆───────────

Christ's Superiority in Hebrews

Instead of the usual salutation, this epistle immediately launches into its theme—the supremacy of Christ even over the Old Testament prophets. Christianity is built upon the highest form of divine disclosure: the personal revelation of God through His incarnate Son. Christ is therefore greater than the prophets, and He is also greater than the angels, as the chart below summarizes.

Jesus Is Greater Than the Prophets (1:1–3)	Jesus Is Greater Than the Angels (1:4–14)
Seven character affirmations:	Seven Scripture quotations:
Heir of all things (v. 2)	Psalm 2:7 (v. 5)
Creator (v. 2)	2 Samuel 7:14 (v. 5)
Manifestation of God's Being (v. 3)	Deuteronomy 32:43 or Psalm 97:7 (v. 6)
Perfect representation of God (v. 3)	Psalm 104:4 (v. 7)
Sustainer of all things (v. 3)	Psalm 45:6, 7 (vv. 8, 9)
Savior (v. 3)	Psalm 102:25–27 (vv. 10–12)
Exalted Lord (v. 3)	Psalm 110:1 (v. 13)

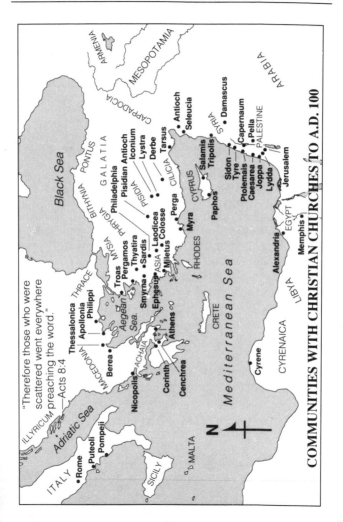

COMMUNITIES WITH CHRISTIAN CHURCHES TO A.D. 100

"Therefore those who were scattered went everywhere preaching the word." —Acts 8:4

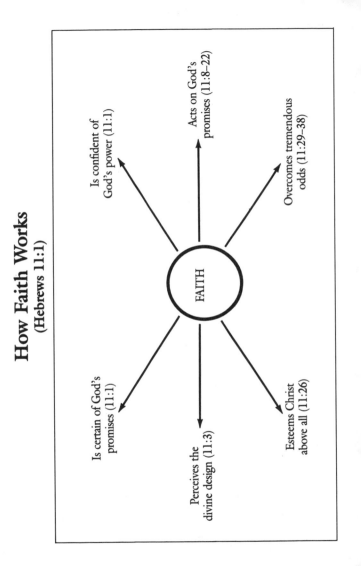

How Faith Works
(Hebrews 11:1)

Is confident of God's power (11:1)

Acts on God's promises (11:8–22)

Overcomes tremendous odds (11:29–38)

Is certain of God's promises (11:1)

FAITH

Perceives the divine design (11:3)

Esteems Christ above all (11:26)

Overview of James

FOCUS	Test of Faith		Characteristics of Faith	Triumph of Faith		
REFERENCE	1:1	1:13	1:19	5:7	5:13	5:19 ——— 5:20
DIVISION	Purpose of Tests	Source of Temptation	Outward Demonstration of Inner Faith	Endures Waiting	Prays for Afflicted	Confronts Sin
TOPIC	Development of Faith		Works of Faith	Power of Faith		
	Response of Faith		Reality of Faith	Reassurance of Faith		
LOCATION	Probably Jerusalem					
TIME	c. A.D. 46–60					

The Hall of Fame of Faith
(Hebrews 11)

The hall of fame of the Scriptures is located in Hebrews 11 and records those who willingly took God at His word even when there was nothing to cling to but His promise.

Person	Scripture Reference
Abel	Genesis 4
Enoch	Genesis 5
Noah	Genesis 6
Abraham	Genesis 12
Jonah	Genesis 17
Isaac	Genesis 27
Jacob	Genesis 48
Joseph	Genesis 50
Moses' parents	Exodus 2
Moses	Exodus 2
Rahab	Joshua 2, 6
Gideon, Barak, Samson, Jephthah	Joshua 4, 6, 13, 11
David, Samuel, and the prophets	1 Samuel

The Epistle of JAMES

◆

LANDMARKS OF JAMES

Key Word: *Faith That Works*

James develops the theme of the characteristics of true faith, using them as a series of tests to help his readers evaluate the quality of their relationship to Christ.

Key Verses: *James 1:19–22 and 2:14–17*

Key Chapter: *James 1*

One of the most difficult areas of the Christian life is that of testings and temptations. James reveals our correct response to both: to testings, count them all joy; to temptations, realize God is not the source.

———————◆———————

A Living Faith
(James)

James wants his readers to demonstrate in their lives the qualities of a living faith. Such a living faith is more than mere knowledge and assent—it includes heartfelt trust that endures and obeys God.

Described as:	Results in:
Tested (1:2, 3)	Patience (1:3)
Without doubt (1:6–8)	Answered prayer (1:5)
Enduring temptation (1:12)	Eternal life (1:12)
More than belief (2:19, 20)	Faith perfected by works (2:22)
Believing God (2:23–25)	Righteousness before God (2:23)

James contrasts living faith to dead, or empty, faith. Dead faith does not result in the transformed life that is characteristic of living faith.

True and Practical Religion

The Epistle of James is a sturdy, compact letter on practical religion. For James, the acid test of true religion is in the doing rather than in the hearing, "believing," or speaking. In this respect James echoes clearly the ethical teaching of Jesus, especially as it is recorded in the Sermon on the Mount (see chart on pp. 304–305).

While some have proposed that James contradicts the great Pauline teaching of justification by faith, Paul as well as James taught that a genuine, living faith results in works of love and obedience. Paul was writing to combat legalism, while James was combatting ethical lethargy (see chart below).

As true faith results in actions, James encourages his readers to patiently endure the sufferings of the present life in view of the future prospect of the coming of the Lord and concludes his epistle with some practical words on prayer and restoration (chapter 5).

Paul and James Compared

	Paul	James
Concern	Legalists	Libertines
Emphasis	Justification with God by faith	Justification (vindication) before men by works
Perspective	Faith as a gift	Faith as genuine
Result	Justified as an eternal postition by believing in Christ	Justified in daily proof by behaving like Christ

James and the Sermon on the Mount

The profound impact of the teaching of Jesus upon James is evident in the many allusions to His teaching, particularly the Sermon on the Mount. Notice the similar teachings, even similar expressions, identified in this chart:

James	Sermon on the Mount	Subject
1:2	Matt. 5:10–12 (Luke 6:22, 23)	Joy in the midst of trials
1:4	Matt. 5:48	God's desire and work in us: perfection
1:5	Matt. 7:7	Asking God for good gifts
1:17	Matt. 7:11	God is the giver of good gifts
1:19, 20	Matt. 5:22	Command against anger
1:22, 23	Matt. 7:24–27	Contrast between hearers and doers (illustrated)
1:26, 27	Matt. 7:21–23	Religious person whose religion is worthless
2:5	Matt. 5:3	The poor as heirs of the kingdom
2:10	Matt. 5:19	The whole moral law to be kept
2:11	Matt. 5:21, 22	Command against murder
2:13	Matt. 5:7; 6:14, 15	The merciful blessed; the unmerciful condemned
2:14–26	Matt. 7:21–23	Dead, worthless (and deceiving) faith
3:12	Matt. 7:16 (Luke 6:44, 45)	Tree producing what is in keeping with its kind

James	Sermon on the Mount	Subject
3:18	Matt. 5:9	Blessing of those who make peace
4:2, 3	Matt. 7:7, 8	Importance of asking God
4:4	Matt. 6:24	Friendship with the world = hostility towards God
4:8	Matt. 5:8	Blessing on and call for the pure in heart
4:9	Matt. 5:4	Blessing and call for those who mourn
4:11, 12	Matt. 7:1–5	Command against wrongly judging others
4:13, 14	Matt. 6:34	Not focusing too much on tomorrow
5:1	(Luke 6:24, 25)	Woe to the rich
5:2	Matt. 6:19, 20	Moth and rust spoiling earthly riches
5:6	(Luke 6:37)	Against condemning the righteous man
5:9	Matt. 5:22; 7:1	Not judging—the judge standing at the door
5:10	Matt. 5:12	The prophets as examples of wrongful suffering
5:12	Matt. 5:33–37	Not making hasty and irreverent oaths

Overview of First Peter

FOCUS	Salvation of the Believer		Submission of the Believer	Suffering of the Believer			
REFERENCE	1:1 ———— 1:13 ————		2:13 ————	3:13 ————	3:18 ————	4:7 ————	5:1 ———— 5:14
DIVISION	Salvation of the Believer	Sanctification of the Believer	Government, Business, Marriage, and All of Life	Conduct in Suffering	Christ's Example of Suffering	Commands in Suffering	Minister in Suffering
TOPIC	Belief of Christians		Behavior of Christians	Buffeting of Christians			
	Holiness		Harmony	Humility			
LOCATION	Either Rome or Babylon						
TIME	c. A.D. 63–64						

The First Epistle of PETER

---◆---

LANDMARKS OF FIRST PETER

Key Word: *Suffering for the Cause of Christ*

The basic theme of 1 Peter is the proper response to Christian suffering. Knowing that his readers will be facing more persecution than ever before, Peter writes to give a divine perspective so that they will be able to endure without wavering.

Key Verses: *First Peter 1:10–12 and 4:12, 13*

Key Chapter: *First Peter 4*

Central in the New Testament revelation concerning how to handle persecution and suffering caused by one's Christian testimony is 1 Peter 4. Christ's suffering to be our model (4:1, 2), but we also are to rejoice in that we can share in His suffering (4:12–14).

---◆---

Christian Behavior in a Pagan Society
(1 Peter 2, 3)

Christians are exhorted to be . . .	Because . . .
Good citizens (2:13, 14)	Foolish men will be silenced (2:15)
Obedient servants (2:18)	Christ in our example (2:21)

A Letter to Christians Abroad

The First Epistle of Peter is addressed to "the pilgrims of the Dispersion in Pontus, Galatia, Cappadocia, Asia, and Bithynia." Writing from Rome, the author encourages them to be strong in the faith as they encounter persecutions.

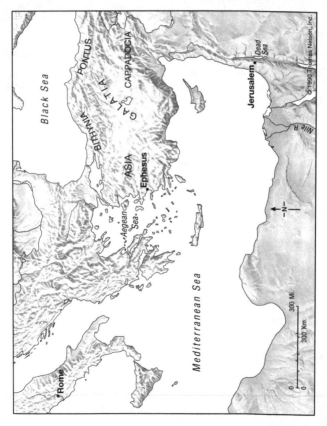

Christians are exhorted to be . . .	Because . . .
Submissive wives (3:1)	Some unbelieving husbands will be won by their example (3:1, 2)
Considerate husbands (3:7)	Their prayers will be heard (3:7)
Compassionate brothers and sisters (3:8)	They will inherit a blessing (3:9)

The Second Epistle to PETER

◆

LANDMARKS OF SECOND PETER

Key Word: *Guard Against False Teachers*

The basic theme that runs through 2 Peter is the contrast between the knowledge and practice of truth versus falsehood.

Key Verses: *Second Peter 1:20, 21 and 3:9–11*

Key Chapter: *Second Peter 1*

The Scripture clearest in defining the relationship between God and man on the issue of inspiration is contained in 1:19–21. Three distinct principles surface:

(1) that the interpretation of Scriptures is not limited to a favored elect but is open for all who "rightly [divide] the word of truth" (2 Tim. 2:15);

(2) that the divinely inspired prophet did not initiate the Scripture himself; and

Overview of Second Peter

FOCUS	Cultivation of Christian Character			Condemnation of False Teachers			Confidence in Christ's Return	
REFERENCE	1:1 ——— 1:15 ———		2:1 ———	2:4 ———	2:10 ———	3:1 ———	3:8 ———	3:18
DIVISION	Growth in Christ	Grounds of Belief	Danger	Destruction	Description	Mockery in the Last Days	Day of the Lord	
TOPIC	True Prophecy		False Prophets			Prophecy: Day of the Lord		
	Holiness		Heresy			Hope		
LOCATION	Probably Rome							
TIME	c. A.D. 64-66 if by Peter; later if by an anonymous author							

(3) that the Holy Spirit (not the emotion or circum-
    stances of the moment) moved holy men.

◆

A Comparison of 1 and 2 Peter

1 Peter	2 Peter
Theme: Hope in the midst of suffering	Theme: The danger of false teaching and practices
Christology: The sufferings of Christ for our salvation and example at His incarnation	Christology: The glory of Christ and the consummation of history at His return
The day of salvation when Christ suffered, died and rose from the dead	The day of the Lord when Christ returns in judgment
Redemptive title: Christ	Title of dominion: Lord
Be encouraged in your present trials	Be warned of eschatological judgment
We need hope to face our trials	We need full knowledge to face error
Numerous similarities to Paul (especially Ephesians and Colossians)	Almost identical similarities to Jude (compart 2 Peter 2 with Jude 4–18)

Overview of First John

FOCUS	Basis of Fellowship		Behavior of Fellowship	
REFERENCE	1:1 ——— 2:15	——— 2:28	——— 5:4	——— 5:21
DIVISION	Conditions for Fellowship	Cautions to Fellowship	Characteristics of Fellowship	Consequences of Fellowship
TOPIC	Meaning of Fellowship		Manifestations of Fellowship	
	Abiding in God's Light		Abiding in God's Love	
LOCATION	Written in Ephesus			
TIME	c. A.D. 90			

The First Epistle of JOHN

---◆---

LANDMARKS OF FIRST JOHN

Key Word: *Fellowship with God*

The major theme of 1 John is fellowship with God. John wants his readers to have assurance of the indwelling God through their abiding relationship with Him (2:28; 5:13). Belief in Christ should be manifested in the practice of righteousness and love for the brethren, which in turn produces joy and confidence before God.

Key Verses: *First John 1:3, 4 and 5:11–13*

Key Chapter: *First John 1*

The two central passages for continued fellowship with God are John 15 and 1 John 1. John 15 relates the positive side of fellowship, that is, abiding in Christ. First John 1 unfolds the other side, pointing out that when Christians do not abide in Christ, they must seek forgiveness before fellowship can be restored.

---◆---

The Quality of Love
(1 John 3–5)

The central theme of John's letter is God—what He is like, how we can fellowship with Him, and the effect that fellowship will have, as the chart below describes (see the chart "The Way of Love," p. 259).

The Source of Love	The Effect of Love
God personifies love (4:8, 16)	We reflect God's love in the world (4:7)
God loved us (4:19)	We love God; our fear is gone; we keep His commands (4:18–19; 5:3)
God gave His Son for us (4:9, 10)	We give our substance for others (3:17; 4:11)
Christ laid down His life for us (3:16)	We lay down our lives for others (3:16)

The Second Epistle of JOHN

◆

LANDMARKS OF SECOND JOHN

Key Word: *Avoid Fellowship with False Teachers*

The basic theme of this brief letter is steadfastness in the practice and purity of the apostolic doctrine that the readers "have heard from the beginning" (v. 6).

Key Verses: *Second John 9, 10*

◆

Comparison of 1, 2, and 3 John

First, Second, and Third John share numerous characteristics in both style and theme. The following chart outlines the major similarities.

Overview of Second John

FOCUS	Abide in God's Commandments			Abide Not with False Teachers		
REFERENCE	1	4	5	7	10	12 ——— 13
DIVISION	Salutation	Walk in Truth	Walk in Love	Doctrine of False Teachers	Avoid the False Teachers	Benediction
		Walk in Commandments			Watch for Counterfeits	
TOPIC		Practice the Truth			Protect the Truth	
LOCATION	Written in Ephesus					
TIME	c. A.D. 90					

Characteristic	1 John	2 John	3 John
Author identified as "the Elder"		v. 1	v. 1
Recipients are those "whom I love in truth"		v. 1	v. 1
Author rejoices because his children "walk in truth"		v. 4	v. 4
Emphasis on "truth"	9 times	11 times	11 times
Reference to "Antichrists" who deny that Jesus Christ has "come in the flesh"	4:3	v. 7	
Genuine love means obedience	5:3	v. 6	
The command to love is not new	2:7 3:11	v. 5 v. 6	
Those who do evil have not seen God	3:6		v. 11

The Third Epistle of
JOHN

◆

LANDMARKS OF THIRD JOHN

Key Word: *Enjoy Fellowship with the Brethren*

The basic theme of this letter is to enjoy and continue to have fellowship (hospitality) with fellow believers, especially full-time Christian workers. This is contrasted between the truth and servanthood of Gaius and the error and selfishness of Diotrephes.

◆

Overview of Third John

FOCUS	Commendation of Gaius			Condemnation of Diotrephes		
REFERENCE	1 ——— 2 ———		5 ———	9 ———	12 ———	13 ——— 14
DIVISION	Salutation	Godliness of Gaius	Generosity of Gaius	Pride of Diotrephes	Praise for Demetrius	Benediction
TOPIC		Servanthood			Selfishness	
	Duty of Hospitality			Danger of Haughtiness		
LOCATION	Written in Ephesus					
TIME	c. A.D. 90					

Walking in Truth
(3 John)

The Third Epistle of John is addressed to Gaius, a man whom John "loves in truth" and who "walks in the truth." His life is a sharp contrast to a man called Diotrephes, whom John describes. The chart below highlights the difference in the two men and two ways of "walking" (see also Psalm 1).

Gaius	Diotrephes
Walks in truth.	Loves to have preeminence
Faithful worker for the truth.	Spreads malicious gossip against John.
Shows hospitality to itinerant Christian ministers.	Refuses to receive the brethren from other assemblies.

The Epistle of
JUDE

◆

LANDMARKS OF JUDE

Key Word: *Contend for the Faith*

This epistle condemns the practices of heretical teachers in the church and counsels the readers to stand firm, grow in their faith, and contend for the truth.

Key Verse: *Jude 3*

◆

Overview of Jude

FOCUS	Purpose	Description of False Teachers				Defense Against False Teachers	Doxology
REFERENCE	1 ——————	5 ——————	8 ——————	14 ——————	17 ——————	24 ——————	25
DIVISION	Introduction	Past Judgment	Present Characteristics	Future Judgment	Duty of Believers	Conclusion	
TOPIC		Reason to Contend			How to Contend		
	Anatomy of Apostasy				Antidote for Apostasy		
LOCATION	Unknown						
TIME	c. A.D. 66–80						

Jesus is Lord
(Jude)

Jude's purpose is clear: The threat of subversive teachers has compelled him to write and exhort his readers "to
contend earnestly for the faith." False teachers reject
Christ's authority, but Jude stresses that Jesus is Lord,
now and forever.

Two Greek words convey this meaning of lord or master, *kyrios* and *despotēs,* and both of them are used to describe Jesus in the New Testament. Some other references
include:

"the only Lord God and Our Lord Jesus Christ"	Jude 4
"My Lord and my God"	John 20:28
"Lord of lords"	1 Tim. 6:15 Rev. 11:15
"the Lord's Day"	Rev. 1:10
"the Lord's Supper"	1 Cor. 11:20
"Prepare the way of the Lord"	Matt. 3:3

The REVELATION
of Jesus Christ

◆

LANDMARKS OF REVELATION
Key Word: *The Revelation of the Coming of Christ*

The purposes for which Revelation was written depend
to some extent on how the book as a whole is interpreted.

(1) The *symbolic or idealist view* maintains that Revelation is not a predictive prophecy, but a symbolic portrait of the cosmic conflict of spiritual principles.

(2) The *preterist view* (the Latin word *praeter* means "past") maintains that it is a symbolic description of the Roman persecution of the church, emperor worship, and the divine judgment of Rome.

(3) The *historicist view* approaches Revelation as an allegorical panorama of the history of the (Western) church from the first century to the Second Advent.

(4) The *futurist view* acknowledges the obvious influence that the first-century conflict between Roman power and the church had upon the themes of this book. It also accepts the bulk of Revelation (chaps. 4—22) as an inspired look into the time immediately preceding the Second Advent (the Tribulation, usually seen as seven years; chaps. 6—18), and extending from the return of Christ to the creation of the new cosmos (chaps. 19—22).

Advocates of all four interpretive approaches to Revelation agree that it was written to assure the recipients of the ultimate triumph of Christ over all who rise up against Him and His saints. The readers were facing dark times of persecution, and even worse times would follow. Therefore they needed to be encouraged to persevere by standing firm in Christ in view of God's plan for the righteous and the wicked.

Key Verses: *Revelation 1:19 and 19:11*

Key Chapters: *Revelation 19—22*

When the end of history is fully understood, its impact radically affects the present. In Revelation 19—22 the

Overview of Revelation

FOCUS	"Things Which You Have Seen"	"Things Which Are"	"Things Which Will Take Place"				
REFERENCE	1:1 ————	2:1 ————	4:1 ————	6:1 ————	19:7 ————	20:1 ————	21:1 ——— 22:21
DIVISION	The Lord Jesus Christ	Seven Churches	The Judge	Tribulation	Second Coming	Millennium	Eternal State
TOPIC	Vision of Christ		Vision of Consummation				
	Theophany	Talks	Tribulations	Tribulations	Trumpets		Together
LOCATION	Written on the Island of Patmos						
TIME	c. A.D. 81–96						

plans of God for the last days and for all of eternity are recorded in explicit terms.

———————————◆———————————

Names for Satan

Satan, or Adversary, is the most frequently used name for the Devil in the New Testament, appearing over fifty times. Devil, or Slanderer, is used over thirty times. Satan, the personification of evil in this world, is the great superhuman enemy of God, His people, and all that is good. Regarded by many scholars as a fallen angel, Satan has a continuing ambition to replace God and have others worship him (Matt. 4:8, 9). He constantly tempts people to try to entice them into sin (1 Thess. 3:5). He sometimes transforms himself into an angel of light (2 Cor. 11:14). Revelation describes the ultimate defeat of the great deceiver (20:1–10). The following chart identifies other titles Scripture uses to refer to this enemy:

Title	Biblical Reference
Beelzebub, ruler of demons	Matt. 12:24
The wicked one	Matt. 13:19
The enemy	Matt. 13:39
Murderer	John 8:44
A liar	John 8:44
Ruler of this world	John 12:31; 14:30
God of this age	2 Cor. 4:4
Prince of the power of the air	Eph. 2:2
Ruler of darkness	Eph. 6:12

THE SEVEN CHURCHES OF REVELATION

Ephesus: the church at the end of the apostolic age (Rev. 2:1–7).

Smyrna: the church under persecution (Rev. 2:8–11).

Pergamos: the church settled in the world (Rev. 2:12–17).

Thyatira: the church in idolatry (Rev. 2:18–29).

Sardis: the church as dead, yet having a believing remnant (Rev. 3:1–6).

Philadelphia: the church in revival (Rev. 3:7–13).

Laodicea: the church in its final state of apostasy (Rev. 3:14–19).

"He who has an ear, let him hear what the Spirit says to the churches."—Rev. 2:11

Title	Biblical Reference
The tempter	1 Thess. 3:5
The king of death	Heb. 2:14
A roaring lion	1 Pet. 5:8
Adversary	1 Pet. 5:8
Angel of the bottomless pit	Rev. 9:11
Abaddon (Destruction)	Rev. 9:11
Apollyon (Destroyer)	Rev. 9:11
The dragon	Rev. 12:7
Accuser of our brethren	Rev. 12:10
Serpent of old	Rev. 20:2
The deceiver	Rev. 20:10

Interpretations of Revelation 20:1–6

In addition to the four major interpretations for all of Revelation summarized in *Landmarks of Revelation,* the reference to the thousand years in Revelation is understood in several ways as well. The key issure is how this thousand years (called "the Millennium," from the Latin word for "thousand") is to be interpreted. The following chart summarizes three options found today among evangelical believers:

Postmillennial	Christ will return *after* the 1,000 years. A golden age on the earth is ushered in by the triumph of the gospel through the church. The 1,000 years is viewed literally by some but symbolically by others.

The Seven Churches of the Apocalypse
(Revelation 2–3)

	Commendation	Criticism	Instruction	Promise
Ephesus (2:1–7)	Rejects evil, perseveres, has patience	Love for Christ no longer fervent	Do the works you did at first	The tree of life
Smyrna (2:8–11)	Gracefully bears suffering	None	Be faithful until death	The crown of life
Pergamos (2:12–17)	Keeps the faith of Christ	Tolerates immorality, idolatry, and heresies	Repent	Hidden manna and a stone with a new name
Thyatira (2:18–29)	Love, service, faith, patience is greater than at first	Tolerates cult of idolatry and immorality	Judgment coming; keep the faith	Rule over nations and receive morning star
Sardis (3:1–6)	Some have kept the faith	A dead church	Repent; strengthen what remains	Faithful honored and clothed in white
Philadelphia (3:7–13)	Perseveres in the faith	None	Keep the faith	A place in God's presence a new name, and the New Jerusalem
Laodicea (3:14–22)	None	Indifferent	Be zealous and repent	Share Christ's throne

Amillennial	There is *no* literal 1,000 years of Christ's reign on the earth.
	Christ is viewed as presently reigning either in: (1) the hearts of men, (2) heaven, or (3) the church.
	The 1,000 years is understood symbolically as representing an extended period of time.
Premillennial	The return of Christ will *precede* the establishment of His literal kingdom on earth.
	Christ and His saints with Him will reign on the earth in fulfillment of O.T. and N.T. prophecy.
	The 1,000 years is understood as predicting a literal future reign of peace and righteousness on the earth.

Index

(m) indicates map

Nelson's Quick-Reference™ Series

Nelson's Quick-Reference™ Bible Concordance

Gives you easy access to over 40,000 key Bible references that are most often sought. Save time and avoid the tedium that goes with wading through long lists of references less sought after. Keyed to the New King James Version, but useful with any.

400 pages / 0-8407-6907-5 / available now

Nelson's Quick-Reference™ Bible Dictionary

More like a "mini-encyclopedia" than a standard dictionary, this compact reference offers an A-Z way to discover fascinating details about the Bible—its characters, history, setting, and doctrines.

784 pages / 0-8407-6906-7 / available now

Nelson's Quick-Reference™ Bible Handbook

Helps you read each of the Bible's 66 books, plus those of the Apocrypha. Offers book introductions, brief summaries, historical and faith-and-life highlights, at-a-glance charts, and detailed teaching outlines. Suggests individual reading plans and schedules for group study.

416 pages / 0-8407-6904-0 / available now

Nelson's Quick-Reference™ Bible Questions and Answers

Learning is fun, lively, and exciting with the over 6,000 questions and answers covering the whole Bible. Variety keeps interest high—short answer, true/false, multiple choice, fill in the blank, and sentence completion.

384 pages / 0-8407-6905-9 / available now

Nelson's Quick-Reference™ Introduction to the Bible

Introduces the Bible as a whole and describes all its parts from an historical and evangelical theological perspective. Explore the fascinating variety in Scripture—story and song, poetry and prophecy, and more. Dis-

cover its divinely revealed answers to the most important questions of life.
384 pages / 0-8407-3206-6 / available now

Nelson's Quick-Reference™
Bible People and Places

From Aaron to Zurishaddain, and from Dan to Beersheba, quickly identify each person and place in the Bible—and many key events. One list, arranged from A to Z, gives brief descriptions and Scripture references, and tells what the names mean, how to say them, and which refer to the same person or place. Variant spellings make this guide useful with any translation.
384 pages / 0-8407-6912-1 / available now

Nelson's Quick-Reference™
Chapter-by-Chapter Bible Commentary

By Warren W. Wiersbe. Supplement your Bible reading with this devotional commentary that spotlights the spiritual and practical truths of Scripture. Drawn from Wiersbe's over forty-five years of study, reflection, and teaching on Scripture, these succinct comments are organized and expressed memorably—a heart-provoking aid to your personal devotions.
864 pages / 0-7852-8235-1 / available now

Nelson's Quick-Reference™
The Life of Christ

By Howard F. Vos. Survey the works and words of the most influential life ever lived—Jesus of Nazareth, the Christ of God. Understand Him in His context by discovering the historical, political, and religious settings in which He lived; and by exploring the Gospels' account of His message, miracles, and complete ministry—the lives He touched and changed by His living, dying, and rising again!
320 pages / 0-8407-3363-1 / available now

Nelson's Quick-Reference™
Introduction to Church History

By Howard F. Vos. Trace the story of the followers of Jesus—from the Upper Room at Pentecost to the ends of the earth as the Christian churches girdle the globe today. Meet the leaders and events that helped spread the Gospel and strengthen the churches. Through this, the most up-to-date introduction to contemporary Christianity worldwide, explore the trends that shape our churches even today.

416 pages / 0-7852-8420-8 / available now